WEEKDAY
MEALS
Oxmoor
House

WELCOME

When I tell folks I learned to cook using a pressure cooker, the usual response is one of shock, followed by a comment like, "Wow! I'm so afraid of those!" However, it was my working mom's logical solution to the challenge of getting a quick, nutritious meal on the table after a hard day at the office, and I quite naturally followed her lead.

But, the Instant Pot® is not my mama's pressure cooker, and coupled with the recipes in *Instant Pot® Weekday Meals*, you can safely make hands-off work of cooking veggies, whole grains, meats, and even dried beans, without soaking, in record time. Whether you need a fast, home-cooked meal, or a slow-cooked, table-ready repast, or just dessert, *Instant Pot® Weekday Meals* has you covered with delicious, made-from-scratch recipes tailored to the Instant Pot®'s state-of-the-art versatility.

Wake up to Steel-Cut Oatmeal with Apples (page 12) or make a big pot of Minestrone Soup (page 63) for dinner, and freeze some for later. Pair Collard Greens with Ham Hocks (page 72) with a wedge of cornbread for quintessential Southern comfort. Impress your company with Chicken Fricassee (page 50), and finish the meal with made-ahead Dulce de Leche Flan (page 92) or elegant Marsala-Poached Pears (page 86). Or, prepare decadent Chocolate-Espresso Pudding Cake (page 84), just because.

I've cleared a permanent place for the Instant Pot® on my kitchen counter, and I know you will too, once you've tasted these wonderful recipes.

Enjoy!

Julie Christopher

Julie Christopher
RECIPE EDITOR

CONTENTS

Spicy Chicken Cacciatore, page 54

INSTANT POT®

STARTER'S GUIDE

What is the Instant Pot®?

The Instant Pot® is a seven-in-one multi-cooker that works as an electric pressure cooker, slow cooker, rice cooker, yogurt maker, steamer, warmer and sauté pan all in one. It cooks meals faster and offers an option for a delayed programmable start time. It saves time cooking foods such as dried beans, stews and meats.

Pressure Cooking in the Instant Pot®

1 Connect power cord. The LED display shows "OFF" indicating that it's in standby state. Follow Cooking Preparations (page 6).

2 Select a cooking function, e.g. [Manual], [Soup], [Meat/Stew], etc. (Steam release handle should be in "Sealing" position.) Once a function key is pressed, its indicator lights up. (Within 10 seconds after pressing a function key, you can still select other function keys or adjust cooking time.)

3 Select cooking pressure. All functions except [Rice] default to "High Pressure." For [Rice] function, the default is "Low Pressure."

4 Select cooking time. You may use the [Adjust] key (except for [Manual] and [Rice] functions) to adjust to default cooking times for each function. Use the [+] or [-] key to fine tune cooking time to the minutes specified in your recipe. Any previously used cooking settings, including fine-tuned times, pressure, and temperature are stored once you change the default settings, even after the Instant Pot® is unplugged. To reset to factory default settings, press and hold the [Adjust] key for 3 seconds when the Instant Pot® is in the "OFF" mode.

5 Cooking starts automatically 10 seconds after the last key press. Three audible beeps will sound to indicate the cooking process has begun. The LED display shows "On" indicating that the pre-heating state is in progress. Once the cooker reaches working pressure, the LED display changes from "On" to the programmed cooking time. The cooking time counts down to indicate the remaining time in minutes.

6 When the pressure cooking cycle finishes, the cooker beeps and automatically goes into the "Keep Warm" cycle, called Auto "Keep Warm" Cycle. Note: Auto "Keep Warm" Cycle is not recommended for rice. (You can deactivate the Auto "Keep Warm" Cycle by pressing a function key twice during initial programming until the [Keep Warm/Cancel] key light goes off.) Pressing the [Keep Warm/Cancel] key at any time will cancel a program, turn the cooker off, and return it to stand-by state.

Slow Cooking in the Instant Pot®

1 Connect the cooker to the power outlet. The LED display shows "OFF" indicating that it's in standby state. Follow Cooking Preparations (page 6).

2 Press the [Slow Cook] function key. (Steam Release Handle should be in "Venting" position.)

3 Change cooking time between 0.5 and 20 hours by pressing the [+] or [-] key.

4 Select the desired cooking mode by repeatedly pressing the [Adjust] key to select temperature ("Less" for LOW; "Normal" for MEDIUM; "More" for HIGH).

5 Cooking starts automatically 10 seconds after the last key is pressed.

6 When the cooking finishes, the cooker beeps and goes into the Auto "Keep Warm" Cycle for 10 hours.

Sautéing

The lid must be off when using the "Sauté " function. Press the [Sauté] key. For safety reasons, the maximum operation time of one "Sauté" cycle is 30 minutes. Select the cooking temperature among "Normal", "More" and "Less" modes with the [Adjust] key. The "Normal" mode is suited for regular sautéing or pan searing. The "More" mode is for stir-frying, blackening meat at a higher temperature, or reducing liquids. The "Less" mode is suitable for simmering liquids, or thickening delicate sauces.

How to Release Pressure

Quick Release:
Turn the steam release handle to the "Venting" position to let out steam until the float valve drops down. Please be aware that Quick Release is not suitable for food with large liquid volume or high starch content (e.g. oatmeal, porridge, sticky liquids, starchy soup, etc.). Food content may splatter out from the steam release. Use Natural Release instead.

Natural Release:
Allow the cooker to cool down naturally until the float valve drops down. This may take 10 to 15 minutes or even longer, depending on the amount of food inside. The cooker will not go into Auto "Keep Warm" Cycle until the pressure has been released.

Instant Pot®
www.InstantPot.com
IP-DUO
Soup
Meat /Stew
Bean /Chili
Poultry
Slow Cook
Sauté
Low Pressure
High Pressure
Less
Normal
More
Pressure
Manual
Adjust
Timer
Rice
Multigrain
Porridge
Steam
Yogurt
Keep Warm /Cancel

COOKING PREPARATIONS

Follow these steps when pressure cooking in the **Instant Pot®** for great results each time.

1 **Open the lid:** Grasp the lid handle, rotate approximately 30 degrees counterclockwise in the direction of "Open" until the ▼ mark on the lid is aligned with the ▲ mark on the cooker base.

2 **Remove the inner pot from cooker:** Except when sautéing, it is easier to add food and liquid to the inner pot while it is out of the cooker. Clean and wipe the outside of the inner pot, and remove objects from inside the cooker before returning the inner pot to the cooker.

3 **Add food and liquid to the inner pot:** For all pressure cooking programs, the total amount of precooked food and liquid should NEVER pass ⅔ of the inner pot capacity. For non-pressure cooking programs, do not fill pass the MAX line.

4 **Close the lid and position the steam release handle properly:** When running any of the programs except "Keep-Warm", "Sauté" or "Slow Cook", align the pointed end of the steam release handle to "Sealing" position. The "Sauté" function must be used without the lid.

5 **Select cooking function, and program the cooker:** Press the desired function key. Adjust pressure, temperature, and cook times according to the directions in your recipe.

Chicken with Rich Lemon-Herb Sauce, page 47

CHAPTER 1

BREAKFAST

PRESSURE COOKER

Ground Corn Breakfast Bowls

SERVES 4 - HANDS-ON: 10 MINUTES
UNDER PRESSURE: 25 MINUTES

Try this "no-stir" method for making creamy grits. Serve with eggs and bacon for a heartier meal.

- **1 cup stone-ground cornmeal**
- **3¾ cups water**
- **1 cup 2% reduced-fat milk**
- **1 tablespoon canola oil**
- **1 garlic clove, chopped**
- **½ teaspoon salt**
- **½ teaspoon Worcestershire sauce**
- **⅛ teaspoon ground red pepper**
- **4 ounces reduced-fat sharp cheddar cheese, shredded (about 1 cup)**
- **¼ cup chopped scallions**

1. Combine cornmeal, 2 cups of the water, milk, oil, and garlic in a 4-cup glass measure. Pour remaining water into inner pot of a 6-quart Instant Pot®. Place the steam rack in cooker. Place the 4-cup glass measure on top of the rack.

2. Close and lock the lid of the Instant Pot®. Turn the steam release handle to "Sealing" position. Press [Manual]; select "High Pressure," and use [-] or [+] to choose 25 minutes pressure cooking time. When time is up, turn cooker off. Open the cooker using Natural Pressure Release (page 4).

3. Stir in salt, Worcestershire sauce, and pepper. Gradually add ¾ cup of the cheese, stirring until cheese melts. Spoon grits from cooker into 4 bowls. Garnish with chopped scallions and remaining shredded cheese.

PRESSURE-PERFECT TIP
For a thinner consistency, stir in 2 to 3 tablespoons additional milk at the end.

Toasted Almond and Apple Quinoa

SERVES 4 - HANDS-ON: 5 MINUTES
UNDER PRESSURE: 6 MINUTES

Jump-start your morning with a bowl of warm quinoa cereal. It's loaded with protein and fiber, which will keep you satisfied throughout the morning.

- **⅔ cup slivered almonds**
- **1 cup uncooked quinoa**
- **2 cups water**
- **⅓ cup dried tart cherries**
- **1 tablespoon canola oil**
- **¼ teaspoon salt**
- **1 teaspoon vanilla extract**
- **1 cup sliced Braeburn apple**
- **1 tablespoon sugar**
- **¼ teaspoon ground cinnamon**

1. Remove lid from a 6-quart Instant Pot®. Press [Sauté], and use [Adjust] to select "Normal" mode. Add almonds to inner pot; cook, stirring constantly, 2 to 3 minutes or until lightly browned. Remove from cooker, and set aside.

2. Add quinoa to cooker; cook 1 minute or until lightly browned, stirring frequently. Stir in 2 cups water and next 3 ingredients (through salt). Turn cooker off.

3. Close and lock the lid of the Instant Pot®. Turn the steam release handle to "Sealing" position. Press [Manual]; select "High Pressure," and use [-] or [+] to choose 6 minutes pressure cooking time. When time is up, turn cooker off. Open the cooker using Natural Pressure Release (page 4). Stir in vanilla.

4. While cooker stands, combine almonds, apple, sugar, and cinnamon, tossing to coat. Divide quinoa mixture among 4 bowls; top with apple mixture.

Peanutty Maple Oats

SERVES 6 - HANDS-ON: 10 MINUTES
UNDER PRESSURE: 3 MINUTES

Peanut butter and maple syrup elevate the flavor and satisfaction of this morning staple.

- **1 cup steel-cut oats**
- **3 cups water**
- **1 tablespoon canola oil**
- **⅛ teaspoon salt**
- **½ cup plus 1 tablespoon reduced-fat peanut butter**
- **1½ cups diced banana**
- **¼ cup pure maple syrup**
- **⅛ teaspoon ground nutmeg**

1. Combine first 4 ingredients (through salt) in a 6-quart Instant Pot®. Close and lock the lid of the Instant Pot®. Turn the steam release handle to "Sealing" position. Press [Manual]; select "High Pressure," and use [-] or [+] to choose 3 minutes pressure cooking time. Open the cooker using Natural Pressure Release (page 4).

2. Stir in peanut butter.

3. Divide oats mixture among 6 bowls. Top with banana, and drizzle with syrup. Sprinkle with nutmeg, and serve immediately.

SWAP IN A SNAP!
Try dried blueberries, cranberries, or raisins in place of the banana—they offer a nice chewy texture.

PRESSURE COOKER

Brown Rice Cereal with Vanilla Cream and Berries

SERVES 4 - HANDS-ON: 10 MINUTES
UNDER PRESSURE: 23 MINUTES

Serve hot, at room temperature, or cold. To make ahead for a breakfast on the go, store in the refrigerator for up to 3 days.

- **1 cup uncooked long-grain brown rice**
- **1½ cups water**
- **1 tablespoon canola oil**
- **1 cup fat-free milk**
- **¼ cup heavy cream**
- **3 tablespoons sugar**
- **⅛ teaspoon salt**
- **1 teaspoon vanilla extract**
- **½ cup fresh blueberries**
- **½ cup fresh raspberries**
- **2 teaspoons grated lemon rind**

1. Remove lid from a 6-quart Instant Pot®. Press [Sauté]; use [Adjust] to select "Normal" mode. When the word "Hot" appears, add rice to inner pot. Cook, stirring constantly, 3 minutes or until lightly toasted. Add 1½ cups water and the oil. Close and lock the lid of the Instant Pot®. Turn the steam release handle to "Sealing" position. Press [Manual]; select "High Pressure," and use [-] or [+] to choose 23 minutes pressure cooking time. When time is up, turn cooker off. Open the cooker using Quick Pressure Release (page 4).

2. Spoon rice from cooker into 4 bowls.

3. Add milk and next 3 ingredients (through salt) to cooker. Press [Sauté]; use [Adjust] to select "Less" mode. Cook, stirring constantly, 2 minutes or until thoroughly heated. Turn cooker off; stir in vanilla.

4. Divide rice among 4 bowls. Top rice with milk mixture. Sprinkle with berries and lemon rind.

Note: For creamier rice, stir milk and next 3 ingredients into cooked rice in cooker. Close and lock the lid of the Instant Pot®. Turn the steam release handle to "Venting" position. Press [Slow Cook], and use [Adjust] to select "Less" mode. Press [-] or [+] to choose 30 minutes cook time. Turn cooker off. Cool slightly and stir in vanilla. Spoon into bowls, and top with berries and lemon rind.

SLOW COOKER

Steel-Cut Oatmeal with Apples

SERVES 10 - HANDS-ON: 3 MINUTES
SLOW COOK: 6 HOURS

While you sleep, your slow cooker is making your breakfast—what could be better?

- **1 teaspoon coconut oil**
- **4 cups diced Granny Smith apple (about 1 pound)**
- **2 cups gluten-free steel-cut oats (such as Bob's Red Mill)**
- **7 cups water**
- **½ cup honey**
- **½ teaspoon salt**
- **½ teaspoon ground allspice**
- **1 (13.66-ounce) can light coconut milk**
- **Toasted cashews (optional)**
- **Additional diced Granny Smith apple (optional)**

Coat the inner pot of a 6-quart Instant Pot® with oil. Combine apple and next 6 ingredients (through coconut milk) in inner pot. Close and lock the lid of the Instant Pot®. Turn the steam release handle to "Venting" position. Press [Slow Cook], and use [Adjust] to select "Less" mode. Press [-] or [+] to choose 6 hours cook time. Stir well before serving. Garnish with toasted cashews and additional diced apple, if desired.

SLOW COOKER

Nut-Seed-Beer Loaf

SERVES 12 - HANDS-ON: 10 MINUTES
SLOW COOK: 2 HOURS

- **¾ cup (about 3 ounces) quinoa flour**
- **¾ cup (about 2.75 ounces) oat flour**
- **1 cup gluten-free old-fashioned rolled oats (such as Bob's Red Mill)**
- **½ cup chopped hazelnuts, toasted**
- **½ cup unsalted sunflower seed kernels, toasted**
- **¼ cup millet**
- **¼ cup psyllium husk powder**
- **1 tablespoon ground chia seeds**
- **1 teaspoon baking powder**
- **¾ teaspoon salt**
- **2 large eggs, lightly beaten**
- **1 cup gluten-free beer (such as Daura Damm)**
- **2 tablespoons coconut oil**
- **2 tablespoons blackstrap molasses**

1. Weigh or lightly spoon flours into dry measuring cups; level with a knife. Combine flours, oats, and next 7 ingredients (through salt) in a medium bowl; stir with a whisk. Combine eggs and next 3 ingredients (through molasses) in a small bowl; stir with a whisk until blended. Add egg mixture to flour mixture, stirring until combined.

2. Remove the inner pot of a 6-quart Instant Pot®. Line bottom and sides of inner pot with parchment paper, folding to fit as needed. Spoon batter onto parchment paper; shape gently into approximately an 8 x 4 x 1½-inch loaf. Tear off a 10½-inch-long piece of aluminum foil; lay foil on top of inner pot, gently smoothing it down the side of the pot. Trim pointed corners even with the rest of the foil, and tightly tuck it in under the rim.

3. Cut 1 (1¼-inch-long) slit in foil about 1 inch from edge with a thin, sharp knife. Cut a second 1¼-inch-long slit parallel to and about 1 inch to the inside of the first. Repeat this procedure 3 times, creating 2 concentric slits in foil at intervals of 12, 3, 6, and 9 o'clock. Set inner pot inside cooker.

4. Close and lock the lid of the Instant Pot®. Turn the steam release handle to "Venting" position. Press [Slow Cook], and use [Adjust] to select "More" mode. Press [-] or [+] to choose 2 hours cook time. When time is up, an instant-read thermometer inserted into center of loaf should register 190°F. (Cook additional time, if necessary.) Turn cooker off.

5. Carefully remove lid from cooker to prevent condensation from dripping onto foil. Blot excess moisture with paper towels, as necessary. Remove foil from inner pot. Remove bread from cooker, and cool completely on a wire rack.

Maple French Toast Casserole

SERVES 8 - HANDS-ON: 8 MINUTES
SLOW COOK: 1 HOUR 30 MINUTES

You can skip standing over a frying pan when you make French toast in a slow cooker. It comes out moist and rich, and is a great way to use up gluten-free bread that has been around for a few days.

- **Cooking spray**
- 12 **(1.3-ounce) slices sandwich bread, cut into 1-inch pieces**
- 4 **large eggs, lightly beaten**
- ½ **cup maple syrup**
- 1 **teaspoon ground cinnamon**
- ¼ **teaspoon salt**
- ¼ **teaspoon grated whole nutmeg**
- ⅛ **teaspoon ground cloves**
- 2 **cups 2% reduced-fat milk**
- 1 **teaspoon powdered sugar**

1. Remove the inner pot of a 6-quart Instant Pot® from the cooker, and coat with cooking spray. Place bread in pot.

2. Combine eggs and next 5 ingredients (through cloves) in a large bowl. Add milk, stirring with a whisk until blended. Pour milk mixture over bread in pot, pressing gently with a spoon to coat all bread pieces.

3. Tear off a 10½-inch-long piece of aluminum foil; lay foil on top of inner pot, gently smoothing it down the side of the pot. Trim pointed corners even with the rest of the foil, and tightly tuck it in under the rim.

4. Cut 1 (1¼-inch-long) slit in foil about 1 inch from edge with a thin, sharp knife. Cut a second 1¼-inch-long slit parallel to and about 1 inch to the inside of the first. Repeat this procedure 3 times, creating 2 concentric slits in foil at intervals of 12, 3, 6, and 9 o'clock. Set inner pot inside cooker.

5. Close and lock the lid of the Instant Pot®. Turn the steam release handle to "Venting" position. Press [Slow Cook], and use [Adjust] to select "More" mode. Press [-] or [+] to choose 1 hour 30 minutes cook time. (Cook additional time, if necessary, until a knife inserted in center comes out clean.) Serve warm sprinkled with powdered sugar.

CHAPTER 2
SOUPS
& STEWS

PRESSURE COOKER

Spanish Chickpea Soup

SERVES 6 - HANDS-ON: 10 MINUTES
UNDER PRESSURE: 1 HOUR 15 MINUTES

Dried chickpeas are typically soaked overnight and then simmered for up to 2½ hours to become tender. These, though, go into the pressure cooker dry and come out tender in just a little over an hour!

8 ounces dried chickpeas (garbanzo beans)
1 tablespoon olive oil
1½ cups chopped onion
4 ounces dry-cured Spanish chorizo, diced
5 garlic cloves, minced
3½ cups water
2½ cups fat-free, lower-sodium chicken broth
2 bay leaves
4 cups baby spinach
1 tablespoon sherry vinegar
½ teaspoon freshly ground black pepper
⅜ teaspoon kosher salt
¼ teaspoon crushed red pepper

1. Sort and wash chickpeas. Remove lid from a 6-quart Instant Pot®. Press [Sauté], and use [Adjust] to select "More" mode. When the word "Hot" appears, swirl in oil. Add onion; cook, stirring constantly, 3 minutes. Add chorizo and garlic; cook, stirring constantly, 2 minutes. Add chickpeas, water, broth, and bay leaves to cooker. Turn cooker off.

2. Close and lock the lid of the Instant Pot®. Turn the steam release handle to "Sealing" position. Press [Manual]; select "High Pressure," and use [-] or [+] to choose 75 minutes pressure cooking time. When time is up, turn cooker off. Open the cooker using Quick Pressure Release (page 4).

3. Remove bay leaves; discard. Add spinach and remaining ingredients, stirring just until spinach wilts. Ladle soup into 6 bowls. Serve immediately.

PRESSURE-PERFECT TIP
Brown the onion, garlic, and sausage before cooking the chickpeas. The browned bits formed on the bottom of the pot give this dish its rich flavor.

PRESSURE COOKER

White Bean, Turkey Sausage, and Tortellini Soup

SERVES 12 - HANDS-ON: 10 MINUTES
UNDER PRESSURE: 29 MINUTES

- **1 tablespoon canola oil**
- **1 pound mild turkey Italian sausage, casings removed**
- **4½ cups water**
- **3½ cups fat-free, lower-sodium chicken broth**
- **1 pound dried navy beans**
- **1 cup chopped fennel bulb**
- **1 teaspoon chopped fresh oregano**
- **1½ cups diced red bell pepper**
- **1 (9-ounce) package fresh three-cheese tortellini**
- **3 cups arugula**
- **¼ cup refrigerated reduced-fat pesto**

1. Remove lid from a 6-quart Instant Pot®. Press [Sauté], and use [Adjust] to select "More" mode. When the word "Hot" appears, swirl in oil. Add sausage, and cook 6 minutes or until browned, stirring to crumble. Drain sausage, and set aside.

2. Add 4½ cups water and broth to cooker, scraping cooker to loosen browned bits. Sort and wash beans. Add beans, fennel, and oregano to cooker. Close and lock the lid of the Instant Pot®. Turn the steam release handle to "Sealing" position. Turn cooker off. Press [Manual]; select "High Pressure," and use [-] or [+] to choose 29 minutes pressure cooking time. When time is up, turn cooker off. Open the cooker using Natural Pressure Release (page 4).

3. With lid off, press [Sauté], and use [Adjust] to select "More" mode. When mixture comes to a boil, stir in cooked sausage, bell pepper, and tortellini. When mixture returns to a boil, turn cooker off. Press [Sauté], and use [Adjust] to select "Normal" mode. Simmer 7 minutes or until tortellini is done. Ladle soup into 12 bowls; top with arugula and pesto.

PRESSURE COOKER

Vegetable Beef Soup

SERVES 12 - HANDS-ON: 25 MINUTES
UNDER PRESSURE: 25 MINUTES

- **1 cup dried navy beans**
- **1 tablespoon olive oil**
- **½ pound boneless chuck eye roast, trimmed and cut into ½-inch cubes**
- **1½ cups chopped onion**
- **1¼ cups sliced carrot**
- **1 cup chopped celery**
- **4 cups lower-sodium beef broth**
- **3 cups water**
- **½ cup uncooked pearl barley**
- **1 teaspoon thyme leaves**
- **¼ teaspoon salt**
- **1 (14.5-ounce) can diced tomatoes with basil, garlic, and oregano, undrained**
- **4 cups thinly sliced kale**
- **1 teaspoon balsamic vinegar**
- **6 teaspoons shredded fresh Parmesan cheese**

1. Sort and wash beans. Remove lid from a 6-quart Instant Pot®. Press [Sauté], and use [Adjust] to select "More" mode. When the word "Hot" appears, swirl in oil. Add beef; cook 3 to 4 minutes or until browned, stirring occasionally. Add onion, carrot, and celery; cook 7 minutes or until vegetables are lightly browned, stirring frequently. Stir in broth and next 5 ingredients (through tomatoes).

2. Turn cooker off. Close and lock the lid of the Instant Pot®. Turn the steam release handle to "Sealing" position. Press [Manual]; select "High Pressure," and use [-] or [+] to choose 25 minutes pressure cooking time. When time is up, open the cooker using Natural Pressure Release (page 4).

3. Add kale and vinegar, stirring until kale wilts. Ladle soup into 12 bowls; sprinkle with cheese.

SWAP IN A SNAP!
Use spinach or chard in place of the kale.

Smoky Pork and Hominy Soup

SERVES 7 - HANDS-ON: 25 MINUTES
UNDER PRESSURE: 40 MINUTES

Try this soup garnished with radish slices and sour cream.

- **4 teaspoons canola oil**
- **2¼ pounds boneless pork shoulder (Boston butt), trimmed and cut into 1-inch pieces**
- **2 cups diced onion**
- **1½ cups water**
- **¼ cup tomato paste**
- **2 tablespoons Spanish smoked paprika**
- **1 tablespoon ground cumin**
- **2 teaspoons dried oregano, crumbled**
- **1½ teaspoons garlic powder**
- **3 (14.5-ounce) cans fat-free, lower-sodium chicken broth**
- **3 (15.5-ounce) cans white hominy, rinsed and drained**
- **1 cup chopped fresh cilantro**

1. Remove lid from a 6-quart Instant Pot®. Press [Sauté], and use [Adjust] to select "More" mode. When the word "Hot" appears, swirl in 2 teaspoons of the oil. Add half of pork to cooker; cook 6 minutes, browning on all sides. Remove pork with a slotted spoon; keep warm. Repeat procedure with remaining oil and remaining pork. Turn cooker off. Return cooked pork to cooker; stir in onion and next 7 ingredients (through broth).

2. Close and lock the lid of the Instant Pot®. Turn the steam release handle to "Sealing" position. Press [Manual]; select "High Pressure," and use [-] or [+] to choose 40 minutes pressure cooking time. When time is up, turn cooker off. Open the cooker using Natural Pressure Release (page 4).

3. With the lid off, press [Sauté], and use [Adjust] to select "More" mode. When mixture comes to a boil, stir in hominy. Cook, uncovered, 10 minutes or until slightly thick, stirring occasionally. Stir in cilantro. Ladle soup into 7 bowls.

Potato, Corn, and Chicken Stew

SERVES 9 - HANDS-ON: 15 MINUTES
UNDER PRESSURE: 23 MINUTES

- **3½ cups fat-free, lower-sodium chicken broth**
- **1½ cups fresh corn kernels (about 3 ears)**
- **1 tablespoon olive oil**
- **4 pounds bone-in chicken thighs, skinned (about 12 thighs)**
- **½ cup chopped onion**
- **½ cup thinly sliced carrot**
- **1½ cups water**
- **2½ cups finely shredded peeled baking potato**
- **2½ cups cubed peeled Yukon gold or red potato**
- **1½ teaspoons chopped fresh oregano**
- **1 teaspoon chopped fresh thyme**
- **¼ cup chopped fresh cilantro**
- **1 tablespoon fresh lime juice**
- **¼ teaspoon salt**
- **½ teaspoon hot pepper sauce (such as Tabasco)**
- **¼ teaspoon freshly ground black pepper**
- **¾ cup cubed peeled avocado**
- **4½ teaspoons capers**

1. Place 1 cup of the broth and ½ cup of the corn in a food processor; process until corn is puréed.

2. Remove lid from a 6-quart Instant Pot®. Press [Sauté], and use [Adjust] to select "More" mode. When the word "Hot" appears, swirl in 1½ teaspoons of the oil. Add half of chicken; cook 5 minutes, browning on all sides. Remove chicken from cooker. Repeat procedure with remaining half of chicken; remove from cooker. Carefully remove inner pot from cooker. Remove drippings from inner pot.

3. Return inner pot to cooker. Add remaining 1½ teaspoons oil to cooker. Add onion and carrot; cook, stirring constantly, 2 minutes. Stir in 1½ cups water and next 4 ingredients (through thyme). Stir in puréed corn mixture, remaining 2½ cups broth, and remaining 1 cup corn. Return chicken thighs to cooker. Turn cooker off.

4. Close and lock the lid of the Instant Pot®. Turn the steam release handle to "Sealing" position. Press [Manual]; select "High Pressure," and use [-] or [+] to choose 23 minutes pressure cooking time. When time is up, open the cooker using Quick Pressure Release (page 4). Remove chicken from cooker; cool slightly.

5. Remove chicken from bones, discarding bones. Shred chicken into bite-sized pieces. Return shredded chicken to cooker. Stir in cilantro and next 4 ingredients (through black pepper). Turn cooker off; press [Sauté], and use [Adjust] to select "More" mode. Cook, uncovered, 5 minutes, or until thoroughly heated, stirring frequently. Ladle stew into 9 bowls; top with avocado and capers.

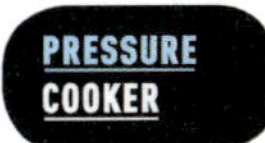

Mexican Chicken Stew

SERVES 8 - HANDS-ON: 5 MINUTES
UNDER PRESSURE: 23 MINUTES

Ground guajillo chile powder found in Mexican markets is quite different from regular chili powder.

- **3 pounds chicken pieces, skinned**
- **2 cups thinly sliced onion**
- **¾ teaspoon salt**
- **½ teaspoon coarsely ground black pepper**
- **3 (14.5-ounce) cans fat-free, lower-sodium chicken broth**
- **4 garlic cloves, crushed**
- **3 bell peppers, seeded and chopped**
- **1 bay leaf**
- **1 (15-ounce) can golden or white hominy, drained**
- **2 tablespoons ground guajillo chile powder**
- **1½ teaspoons dried oregano**
- **½ cup roasted unsalted pumpkinseed kernels**
- **¼ cup chopped fresh cilantro**
- **¼ cup sliced radishes**
- **¼ cup sliced scallions**
- **½ cup crumbled queso fresco cheese**

1. Combine first 8 ingredients (through bay leaf) in a 6-quart Instant Pot®. Close and lock the lid of the Instant Pot®. Turn the steam release handle to "Sealing" position. Press [Manual]; select "High Pressure," and use [-] or [+] to choose 23 minutes pressure cooking time. When time is up, open the cooker using Quick Pressure Release (page 4). Remove chicken from broth mixture; cool slightly. Remove chicken from bones; cut chicken into bite-sized pieces. Discard bones.

2. Strain stock through a sieve over a bowl; discard solids. Return inner pot to cooker; return stock to inner pot. Stir in chicken, hominy, chile powder, and oregano. Let stand 5 minutes. Skim fat from surface of broth; discard.

3. Ladle stew into 8 bowls; top each serving evenly with pumpkin-seed kernels, cilantro, radishes, scallions, and queso fresco cheese.

PRESSURE COOKER

Chicken-Barley Soup

SERVES 6 - HANDS-ON: 10 MINUTES
UNDER PRESSURE: 19 MINUTES

Using chicken stock guarantees more flavor than traditional broth and a nicer golden color in the soup.

- **3 cups unsalted chicken stock**
- **2 cups water**
- **2 cups diced carrot**
- **1 cup diced peeled Yukon gold or red potato**
- **1 cup diced onion**
- **¾ cup sliced celery**
- **½ cup uncooked pearl barley**
- **1 tablespoon chopped fresh oregano**
- **½ teaspoon salt**
- **½ teaspoon freshly ground black pepper**
- **1 bay leaf**
- **2 cups shredded skinless, boneless rotisserie chicken breast**
- **Additional chopped fresh oregano (optional)**
- **Additional freshly ground black pepper (optional)**

1. Combine first 11 ingredients (through bay leaf) in a 6-quart Instant Pot®. Close and lock the lid of the Instant Pot®. Turn the steam release handle to "Sealing" position. Press [Manual]; select "High Pressure," and use [-] or [+] to choose 19 minutes pressure cooking time. When time is up, turn cooker off. Open the cooker using Natural Pressure Release (page 4). Remove and discard bay leaf.

2. Add chicken to cooker. Press [Sauté], and use [Adjust] to select "More" mode. Cook, uncovered, 3 minutes or until thoroughly heated, stirring occasionally. Ladle soup into 6 bowls. Sprinkle with additional oregano and pepper, if desired.

PRESSURE COOKER

Red Pepper Soup with Gouda

SERVES 6 - HANDS-ON: 10 MINUTES
UNDER PRESSURE: 6 MINUTES

- **4 red bell peppers (about 1½ pounds), halved**
- **1 tablespoon canola oil**
- **1 cup diced onion**
- **½ cup sliced carrot**
- **½ cup sliced celery**
- **½ teaspoon garlic powder**
- **1 (14.5-ounce) can organic vegetable broth**
- **1 (15.5-ounce) can unsalted navy beans, rinsed and drained**
- **1 chipotle chile, canned in adobo sauce**
- **1 teaspoon adobo sauce**
- **1 cup half-and-half**
- **1 ounce Gouda cheese, shredded (about ¼ cup)**

1. Thinly slice 3 bell pepper halves, and chop 2 bell pepper halves; set aside remaining bell pepper halves and chopped bell pepper. Remove lid from a 6-quart Instant Pot®. Press [Sauté], and use [Adjust] to select "More" mode. When the word "Hot" appears, swirl in oil. Add sliced bell pepper to cooker; cook, stirring constantly, 5 minutes or until browned. Turn cooker off.

2. Stir in remaining 3 bell pepper halves, onion, and next 7 ingredients (through adobo sauce). Close and lock the lid of the Instant Pot®. Turn the steam release handle to "Sealing" position. Press [Manual]; select "High Pressure," and use [-] or [+] to choose 6 minutes pressure cooking time. When time is up, turn cooker off. Open the cooker using Natural Pressure Release (page 4). Remove inner pot from cooker; cool soup 15 minutes.

3. Place half of pepper mixture in a blender. Remove center piece of blender lid (to allow steam to escape); secure blender lid on blender. Place a clean towel over opening in blender lid (to avoid splatters). Blend until smooth. Pour into a large bowl. Repeat procedure with remaining pepper mixture. Return puréed mixture to inner pot. Return inner pot to cooker. Stir in half-and-half. Press [Sauté], and use [Adjust] to select "More" mode. Cook, uncovered, 2 to 3 minutes or until thoroughly heated. Ladle soup into 6 bowls; sprinkle with cheese and chopped bell pepper.

PRESSURE COOKER

Cauliflower Soup with Shiitakes

SERVES 4 - HANDS-ON: 10 MINUTES
UNDER PRESSURE: 4 MINUTES

- **4 teaspoons olive oil**
- **¾ cup thinly sliced leek, white and light green parts only**
- **⅜ teaspoon kosher salt**
- **4 cups coarsely chopped cauliflower florets (about 1 medium head)**
- **1½ cups unsalted chicken stock (such as Swanson)**
- **¾ cup water**
- **2 teaspoons chopped fresh thyme**
- **¼ cup 2% reduced-fat milk**
- **1½ teaspoons butter**
- **¼ teaspoon white pepper**
- **1 (3.5-ounce) package shiitake mushroom caps**
- **1 teaspoon lower-sodium Worcestershire sauce**
- **1 teaspoon sherry vinegar**
- **2 teaspoons chopped fresh parsley**

1. Remove lid from a 6-quart Instant Pot®. Press [Sauté], and use [Adjust] to select "More" mode. When the word "Hot" appears, swirl in 2 teaspoons of the oil. Add leek; cook, stirring constantly, 1 minute. Add ⅛ teaspoon of the salt. Cook 5 minutes or until leeks are softened, stirring occasionally. Add cauliflower, 1 cup and 6 tablespoons of the stock, ¾ cup water, and thyme. Turn cooker off.

2. Close and lock the lid of the Instant Pot®. Turn the steam release handle to "Sealing" position. Press [Manual]; select "High Pressure," and use [-] or [+] to choose 4 minutes pressure cooking time. When time is up, turn cooker off. Open the cooker using Quick Pressure Release (page 4). Remove inner pot from cooker.

3. Place cauliflower mixture in a blender. Remove center piece of blender lid (to allow steam to escape); secure blender lid on blender. Place a clean towel over opening in blender lid (to avoid splatters). Blend until smooth. Return to inner pot. Stir in remaining ¼ teaspoon salt, milk, butter, and pepper. Return inner pot to cooker. Press [Keep Warm].

4. Thinly slice mushroom caps. Heat a large skillet over medium-high heat. Add remaining 2 teaspoons oil to pan, and swirl to coat. Add mushrooms; sauté 6 minutes or until browned. Add remaining 2 tablespoons stock, Worcestershire sauce, and sherry vinegar. Cook 1 minute or until liquid is reduced and syrupy.

5. Ladle soup evenly into 4 bowls. Top each serving with mushroom mixture. Sprinkle evenly with parsley.

Spicy Black Bean Soup with Chorizo

SERVES 8 - HANDS-ON: 10 MINUTES
SLOW COOK: 8 HOURS

Dried beans don't have to be soaked—just toss them into the Instant Pot®.

- **2 cups chopped onion**
- **1 cup chopped Cuban green peppers or green bell peppers**
- **4 cups fat-free, lower-sodium chicken broth**
- **2 cups water**
- **¼ cup minced jalapeño pepper**
- **2 teaspoons Spanish smoked paprika**
- **1 teaspoon ground cumin**
- **1 teaspoon dried oregano**
- **½ teaspoon salt**
- **½ teaspoon hot pepper sauce (such as Tabasco)**
- **1 pound dried black beans, sorted and rinsed**
- **3 ounces dry-cured Spanish chorizo, diced**
- **4 garlic cloves, minced**
- **1 bay leaf**
- **Reduced-fat sour cream (optional)**
- **Diced onion (optional)**
- **Chopped fresh cilantro (optional)**

Combine first 14 ingredients (through bay leaf) in the inner pot of a 6-quart Instant Pot®. Close and lock the lid of the Instant Pot®. Turn the steam release handle to "Venting" position. Press [Slow Cook], and use [Adjust] to select "Less" mode. Press [-] or [+] to choose 8 hours cook time. Turn cooker off. Skim fat from surface of cooking liquid. Discard bay leaf. Partially mash beans with back of spoon. Ladle soup into 8 bowls. Serve with sour cream, diced onion, and cilantro, if desired.

Spicy Chicken and Butternut Squash Tortilla Soup

Stirring tortilla strips into the soup helps thicken the broth and lends an earthy flavor to the dish.

SERVES 6 - HANDS-ON: 18 MINUTES
SLOW COOK: 8 HOURS

- **1½ pounds bone-in chicken thighs, skinned (about 4 thighs)**
- **1 tablespoon salt-free southwest chipotle seasoning (such as Mrs. Dash)**
- **½ teaspoon kosher salt**
- **1 teaspoon olive oil**
- **2 cups thinly sliced celery stalks and leaves**
- **1½ cups chopped red onion**
- **⅓ cup thinly sliced jalapeño pepper**
- **1 tablespoon minced fresh garlic**
- **1 teaspoon ground cumin**
- **1 (32-ounce) carton chicken stock (such as Kitchen Basics)**
- **3 cups cubed peeled butternut squash**
- **2 bay leaves**
- **6 (6-inch) corn tortillas**
- **Cooking spray**
- **⅛ teaspoon ground red pepper**
- **Sliced jalapeño pepper (optional)**

1. Sprinkle chicken with seasoning and salt. Remove lid from a 6-quart Instant Pot®. Press [Sauté]; use [Adjust] to select "More" mode. When the word "Hot" appears, swirl in oil. Add chicken to inner pot; cook 5 minutes, browning on all sides. Remove chicken from pot. Add celery, onion, and jalapeño pepper to drippings; cook, stirring constantly, 4 minutes. Add garlic and cumin; cook, stirring constantly, 1 minute. Stir in 1 cup of the stock, scraping pot to loosen browned bits. Stir in remaining stock, squash, and bay leaves; add chicken. Turn cooker off.

2. Close and lock the lid of the Instant Pot®. Turn the steam release handle to "Venting" position. Press [Slow Cook], and use [Adjust] to select "Less" mode. Press [-] or [+] to choose 8 hours cook time. When time is up, remove chicken from inner pot with a slotted spoon; cool slightly. Remove and discard bay leaves.

3. While chicken cools, cut tortillas in half; cut tortilla halves crosswise into thin strips to measure 1¾ cups. Heat a large well-seasoned cast-iron skillet over medium-high heat. Coat tortilla strips with cooking spray, and sprinkle with red pepper. Add tortilla strips to skillet; cook 5 to 6 minutes or until crisp, stirring frequently. Remove from heat.

4. Remove chicken from bones; cut meat into bite-sized pieces. Discard bones. Return chicken meat to inner pot; stir in half of tortilla strips. Ladle soup into 6 bowls; top with remaining tortilla strips and, if desired, jalapeño slices.

Butternut Squash Soup

If your supermarket sells pre-cut butternut squash, consider picking it up to save time on prep.

SERVES 8 - HANDS-ON: 10 MINUTES
SLOW COOK: 6 HOURS

8 cups (1½-inch) cubed peeled butternut squash (about 2¼ pounds)
4 cups unsalted chicken stock
½ cup chopped onion
1 tablespoon minced peeled fresh ginger
¾ teaspoon salt
¼ teaspoon ground nutmeg
¼ teaspoon freshly ground black pepper
2 garlic cloves, minced
1 bay leaf
Thyme leaves (optional)

1. Combine all ingredients except thyme leaves in inner pot of a 6-quart Instant Pot®. Close and lock the lid of the Instant Pot®. Turn the steam release handle to "Venting" position. Press [Slow Cook], and use [Adjust] to select "Less" mode. Press [-] or [+] to choose 6 hours cook time. When time is up, turn cooker off. Remove lid. Discard bay leaf.

2. Purée squash mixture with an immersion blender until smooth. Ladle soup into bowls. Garnish with thyme leaves, if desired.

Butternut Squash Soup

Curried Squash and Apple Soup

SERVES 8 - HANDS-ON: 20 MINUTES
SLOW COOK: 8 HOURS

3 cups cubed peeled butternut squash (2 pounds)
2 cups diced peeled apple (2 medium)
2 cups chopped onion (about 1 large)
3 cups fat-free, lower-sodium chicken broth
2 teaspoons minced fresh garlic
1½ teaspoons grated peeled fresh ginger
1 teaspoon red curry powder
½ teaspoon salt
½ teaspoon ground coriander
½ teaspoon freshly ground black pepper

1. Combine all ingredients in the inner pot of a 6-quart Instant Pot®. Close and lock the lid of the Instant Pot®. Turn the steam release handle to "Venting" position. Press [Slow Cook], and use [Adjust] to select "Less" mode. Press [-] or [+] to choose 8 hours cook time. When time is up, turn cooker off. Remove lid.

2. Place half of squash mixture in a blender. Remove center piece of blender lid (to allow steam to escape); secure blender lid on blender. Place a clean towel over opening in blender lid (to avoid splatters). Blend until smooth. Pour into a large bowl. Repeat procedure with remaining squash mixture. Ladle soup into 8 bowls.

Wild Mushroom Soup

SERVES 12 - HANDS-ON: 30 MINUTES
SLOW COOK: 4 HOURS

Marsala, a fortified wine from Sicily, gives this soup wonderful flavor. Feel free to substitute sherry for a similar effect.

- **2 cups boiling water**
- **1¼ cups dried porcini mushrooms (about 1½ ounces)**
- **2 cups water**
- **1 tablespoon cornstarch**
- **2 teaspoons gluten-free reduced-sodium tamari soy sauce**
- **½ teaspoon salt**
- **½ teaspoon freshly ground black pepper**
- **2 tablespoons olive oil**
- **2 cups sliced shallots (about 8 ounces)**
- **1 garlic clove, minced**
- **1 cup dry Marsala or Madeira**
- **2 teaspoons chopped fresh thyme**
- **3 pounds assorted mushrooms (such as cremini, portobello, shiitake, and button), sliced**
- **Chopped fresh parsley (optional)**

1. Pour 2 cups boiling water over porcini mushrooms. Let stand 20 minutes. Drain porcini mushrooms in a colander over a bowl, reserving mushroom broth. Strain mushroom broth through a cheesecloth-lined colander into a bowl; discard solids. Add 2 cups water and next 4 ingredients (through pepper) to mushroom broth; set aside.

2. Remove lid from a 6-quart Instant Pot®. Press [Sauté]; use [Adjust] to select "More" mode. When the word "Hot" appears, swirl in oil. Add shallots and garlic; cook, stirring constantly, 4 to 5 minutes or until shallots are soft. Stir in Marsala. When mixture comes to a boil, cook 30 seconds. Turn cooker off.

3. Add porcini mushrooms, broth mixture, thyme, and sliced mushrooms. Close and lock the lid of the Instant Pot®. Turn the steam release handle to "Venting" position. Press [Slow Cook], and use [Adjust] to select "More" mode. Press [-] or [+] to choose 4 hours cook time. Ladle soup into 12 bowls. Garnish with parsley, if desired.

Smoked Pork and Split Pea Soup

SERVES 8 - HANDS-ON: 22 MINUTES
SLOW COOK: 8 HOURS

An immersion blender is handy for puréeing this soup.

1 pound green split peas
6 whole allspice
3 cardamom pods
1 star anise
1 cup chopped onion
1 cup finely chopped carrot
7 cups water
¼ cup fresh orange juice
¼ cup dry sherry
1 teaspoon dried thyme
1 teaspoon freshly ground black pepper
½ teaspoon salt
½ teaspoon ground cumin
3 garlic cloves, chopped
1 ham hock (about ½ pound)
1 bay leaf
15 ounces smoked pork chops, trimmed and diced (about 2 cups)
1 teaspoon grated orange rind

1. Sort and wash peas; place in a large Dutch oven.

2. Place allspice, cardamom pods, and star anise on a double layer of cheesecloth. Gather edges of cheesecloth together; tie securely, and place in inner pot of a 6-quart Instant Pot®. Add peas, onion, and next 11 ingredients (through bay leaf). Close and lock the lid of the Instant Pot®. Turn the steam release handle to "Venting" position. Press [Slow Cook], and use [Adjust] to select "Less" mode. Press [-] or [+] to choose 5 hours cook time.

3. When time is up, remove lid. Turn cooker off. Add diced pork. Close and lock the lid of the Instant Pot®. Turn the steam release handle to "Venting" position. Press [Slow Cook], and use [Adjust] to select "Less" mode. Press [-] or [+] to choose 3 hours cook time. Cook additional time, if necessary, until peas and pork are tender.

4. Remove lid. Discard bay leaf, spice bag, and ham hock. Place half of soup mixture in a blender. Remove center piece of blender lid (to allow steam to escape); secure blender lid on blender. Place a clean towel over opening in blender lid (to avoid splatters). Blend until smooth. Return puréed mixture to remaining soup in cooker. Stir in orange rind before serving. Ladle soup into 8 bowls.

Spiced Turkey-Chickpea Chili

SERVES 8 - HANDS-ON: 8 MINUTES
SLOW COOK: 6 HOURS

- **1 cup chopped orange bell pepper**
- **2 cups fat-free, lower-sodium chicken broth**
- **½ cup dry white wine**
- **¼ cup minced seeded jalapeño pepper**
- **1 teaspoon chili powder**
- **½ teaspoon Berbere seasoning**
- **½ teaspoon ground turmeric**
- **¼ teaspoon ground red pepper**
- **¼ teaspoon ground cinnamon**
- **1 pound lean ground turkey**
- **1 (14.5-ounce) can diced tomatoes, drained**
- **¾ pound dried chickpeas (garbanzo beans)**
- **1 (8-ounce) can lower-sodium tomato sauce**
- **3 large garlic cloves, minced**
- **½ teaspoon salt**
- **Sour cream (optional)**
- **Chopped fresh cilantro (optional)**

1. Combine first 14 ingredients (through garlic) in inner pot of a 6-quart Instant Pot®. Close and lock the lid of the Instant Pot®. Turn the steam release handle to "Venting" position. Press [Slow Cook], and use [Adjust] to select "Less" mode. Press [-] or [+] to choose 6 hours cook time.

2. When time is up, remove lid, and stir well to crumble turkey. Stir in salt. Ladle chili into 8 bowls, and top with sour cream and cilantro, if desired.

CHAPTER 3

MEATS

PRESSURE COOKER

Beef Bourguignon

SERVES 7 - HANDS-ON: 10 MINUTES
UNDER PRESSURE: 23 MINUTES

This classic French stew is perfect cold-weather fare and is delicious over noodles or mashed potatoes.

¼ cup (about 1.1 ounces) all-purpose flour
½ teaspoon salt
½ teaspoon freshly ground black pepper
1½ pounds boneless chuck roast, trimmed and cut into 1-inch cubes
2 bacon slices, diced
½ cup dry red wine
1 (10½-ounce) can beef broth
3 cups baby carrots (about ¾ pound)
2 cups sliced shiitake mushroom caps (about ½ pound)
2 teaspoons dried thyme
6 shallots, halved (about ½ pound)
4 garlic cloves, thinly sliced
7 cups hot cooked medium egg noodles (about 5 cups uncooked pasta)
Thyme leaves (optional)

1. Weigh or lightly spoon flour into a dry measuring cup; level with a knife. Combine flour, salt, and pepper in a large zip-top plastic bag. Add beef; seal and shake to coat.

2. Remove lid from a 6-quart Instant Pot®. Press [Sauté], and use [Adjust] to select "More" mode. Place bacon in cooker, and cook, stirring constantly, 30 seconds. Add half of beef mixture to cooker; cook 5 minutes, browning on all sides. Remove beef and bacon from cooker. Repeat procedure with remaining beef mixture. Turn cooker off. Return cooked beef and bacon to cooker. Stir in wine and broth, scraping inner pot to loosen browned bits. Add carrots and next 4 ingredients (through garlic).

3. Close and lock the lid of the Instant Pot®. Turn the steam release handle to "Sealing" position. Press [Manual]; select "High Pressure," and use [-] or [+] to choose 23 minutes pressure cooking time. When time is up, turn cooker off. Open the cooker using Quick Pressure Release (page 4). Serve beef mixture over noodles. Garnish with thyme leaves, if desired.

SWAP IN A SNAP!
Portobello mushrooms make a good substitute for the shiitake variety.

Cabernet-Braised Beef Short Ribs

SERVES 6 - HANDS-ON: 10 MINUTES
UNDER PRESSURE: 52 MINUTES

Cooking short ribs in red wine will deliver an unbelievably rich sauce perfect for spooning over noodles. Serve with a chunk of bread to soak up all the sauce.

- **4 tablespoons all-purpose flour**
- **2 pounds bone-in beef short ribs, trimmed**
- **½ teaspoon salt**
- **½ teaspoon freshly ground black pepper**
- **1 tablespoon olive oil**
- **1½ cups (1-inch-thick) sliced celery**
- **1 cup (1-inch-thick) sliced carrot**
- **6 garlic cloves, sliced**
- **2 (6-inch) rosemary sprigs**
- **1 medium onion, cut into 8 wedges**
- **2 tablespoons tomato paste**
- **½ cup fat-free, lower-sodium beef broth**
- **½ cup cabernet sauvignon or other dry red wine**
- **¼ cup water**
- **1 tablespoon cold water**
- **3 cups hot cooked wide egg noodles**
- **Chopped fresh parsley (optional)**

1. Place 3 tablespoons flour in a shallow dish. Sprinkle beef with salt and pepper; dredge in flour. Remove lid from a 6-quart Instant Pot®. Press [Sauté], and use [Adjust] to select "More" mode. When the word "Hot" appears, swirl in oil. Add beef to cooker; cook 8 minutes, browning on all sides. Remove beef from cooker, reserving 1 tablespoon drippings in cooker.

2. Add celery and next 4 ingredients (through onion) to drippings in cooker; sauté 4 minutes. Stir in tomato paste. Add broth, wine, and ¼ cup water to cooker, scraping cooker to loosen browned bits. Return ribs to cooker. Turn cooker off.

3. Close and lock the lid of the Instant Pot®. Turn the steam release handle to "Sealing" position. Press [Manual]; select "High Pressure," and use [-] or [+] to choose 52 minutes pressure cooking time. When time is up, turn cooker off. Open the cooker using Quick Pressure Release (page 4).

4. Remove beef from cooker. Strain cooking liquid through a fine sieve into a bowl; discard solids. Return cooking liquid to cooker. With lid off, press [Sauté], and use [Adjust] to select "More" mode.

5. Combine 1 tablespoon cold water and 1 tablespoon flour in a small bowl. When cooking liquid comes to a boil, add flour mixture, stirring with a whisk. Turn cooker off. Press [Sauté], and use [Adjust] to select "Normal" mode. Simmer, stirring constantly, 3 minutes or until slightly thick. Serve ribs and noodles with sauce. Garnish with chopped parsley, if desired.

Spaghetti and Meatballs with Red Wine

SERVES 6 - HANDS-ON: 15 MINUTES
UNDER PRESSURE: 6 MINUTES

No more waiting hours for homemade meatballs! Have these on the table for dinner, even on a busy weeknight, in about 30 minutes.

- **1 pound extra-lean ground beef**
- **⅔ cup finely chopped onion**
- **½ cup panko (Japanese breadcrumbs)**
- **1.5 ounces grated fresh Parmesan or Asiago cheese (about 6 tablespoons)**
- **3 tablespoons oregano leaves**
- **1 teaspoon dried fennel seed**
- **2 teaspoons minced fresh garlic**
- **½ teaspoon crushed red pepper**
- **1 large egg, lightly beaten**
- **1 tablespoon canola oil**
- **½ cup dry red wine**
- **2 teaspoons sugar**
- **1 (28-ounce) can crushed tomatoes, undrained**
- **12 ounces uncooked multigrain spaghetti (such as Barilla Plus)**
- **Oregano leaves (optional)**

1. Combine beef, ⅓ cup of the onion, panko, cheese, 1½ tablespoons of the oregano, fennel seed, 1 teaspoon of the garlic, ¼ teaspoon of the crushed red pepper, and egg in a medium bowl. Shape mixture into 24 meatballs (about 1 tablespoon each).

2. Remove lid from a 6-quart Instant Pot®. Press [Sauté], and use [Adjust] to select "More" mode. When the word "Hot" appears, swirl in oil. Add remaining ⅓ cup onion and 1 teaspoon garlic; cook, stirring constantly, 3 to 4 minutes or just until tender. Stir in wine, scraping cooker to loosen browned bits. Stir in remaining 1½ tablespoons oregano, remaining ¼ teaspoon crushed red pepper, and sugar. Arrange meatballs in a single layer in cooker; top with tomatoes (do not stir). Turn cooker off.

3. Close and lock the lid of the Instant Pot®. Turn the steam release handle to "Sealing" position. Press [Manual]; select "High Pressure," and use [-] or [+] to choose 6 minutes pressure cooking time. When time is up, open the cooker using Quick Pressure Release (page 4).

4. While meatballs cook, cook spaghetti according to package directions, omitting salt and fat; drain. Serve meatballs and tomato sauce over spaghetti. Sprinkle with oregano leaves, if desired.

Kalamata and Sun-Dried Tomato Brisket

SERVES 8 - HANDS-ON: 15 MINUTES
UNDER PRESSURE: 52 MINUTES

Try this saucy beef over pasta, rice, or potatoes, or on top of crusty Italian whole-grain bread slices for open-faced sandwiches.

- **2 teaspoons canola oil**
- **1 (2½-pound) beef brisket, trimmed and cut in half**
- **8 medium shallots, peeled and halved**
- **2 cups dry red wine**
- **1½ tablespoons Worcestershire sauce**
- **1 (8-ounce) can tomato sauce**
- **⅓ cup thinly sliced sun-dried tomato halves**
- **1 teaspoon dried oregano**
- **1 teaspoon garlic powder**
- **½ cup chopped pitted kalamata olives**
- **¼ teaspoon salt**
- **Chopped fresh parsley (optional)**

1. Remove lid from a 6-quart Instant Pot®. Press [Sauté], and use [Adjust] to select "More" mode. When the word "Hot" appears, swirl in 1 teaspoon of the oil. Add half of brisket to cooker; cook 2 minutes on each side or until browned. Remove from cooker. Repeat procedure with remaining 1 teaspoon oil and remaining brisket half. Add shallots to drippings in cooker; sauté 2 minutes or until lightly browned. Stir in wine, Worcestershire sauce, and tomato sauce. Add brisket halves and any accumulated juices, sun-dried tomatoes, oregano, and garlic powder.

2. Turn cooker off. Close and lock the lid of the Instant Pot®. Turn the steam release handle to "Sealing" position. Press [Manual]; select "High Pressure," and use [-] or [+] to choose 52 minutes pressure cooking time. When time is up, turn cooker off. Open the cooker using Natural Pressure Release (page 4).

3. Remove brisket from cooker; let stand 5 minutes. Cut brisket diagonally across grain into thin slices. Add olives and salt to cooking liquid in cooker. Spoon cooking liquid over brisket before serving; sprinkle with parsley, if desired.

SWAP IN A SNAP!
Quarter one red onion, and use in place of the shallots.

Pork Carnitas Tacos

SERVES 7 - HANDS-ON: 25 MINUTES
UNDER PRESSURE: 29 MINUTES

Pork shoulder, quick-braised with orange juice and spices in the pressure cooker, and then broiled to crispy perfection, provides the base for our Pork Carnitas Tacos. For a lower carb count, swap lettuce cups for the corn tortillas.

- **1½ cups fresh orange juice**
- **1 cup thinly sliced onion**
- **5 teaspoons chipotle chile powder**
- **1 tablespoon ground cumin**
- **1 teaspoon kosher salt**
- **6 garlic cloves, minced**
- **3 pounds boneless pork shoulder (Boston butt), trimmed and cut into 2-inch pieces**
- **14 (6-inch) corn tortillas**
- **2½ cups chopped tomato**
- **½ cup cilantro leaves**
- **Lime wedges (optional)**

1. Combine first 6 ingredients (through garlic) in a 6-quart Instant Pot®. Add pork, tossing to coat. Close and lock the lid of the Instant Pot®. Turn the steam release handle to "Sealing" position. Press [Manual]; select "High Pressure," and use [-] or [+] to choose 29 minutes pressure cooking time. When time is up, turn cooker off. Open the cooker using Natural Pressure Release (page 4).

2. Remove pork from cooker with a slotted spoon; shred with 2 forks to measure 4¾ cups meat. Remove and discard any chunks of fat. Spread pork in a single layer on a jelly-roll pan or broiler pan lined with foil.

3. Skim fat from cooking liquid in cooker; discard fat. With lid off, press [Sauté], and use [Adjust] to select "More" mode. When cooking liquid comes to a boil, turn cooker off. Press [Sauté], and use [Adjust] to select "Normal" mode. Simmer, uncovered, 5 minutes or until slightly thick, stirring frequently.

4. Preheat broiler.

5. Drizzle pork with ¼ cup cooking liquid. Discard remaining cooking liquid, or set aside for serving, if desired. Broil pork 3 to 5 minutes or until pork is browned and edges are crispy, turning pork occasionally.

6. Heat tortillas in microwave according to package directions. Spoon ⅓ cup shredded pork mixture onto each tortilla. Top each with about 3 tablespoons tomato and about 1½ teaspoons cilantro. Serve with lime wedges, if desired.

PRESSURE-PERFECT TIP
Cut the pork into uniform pieces so that it cooks evenly.

PRESSURE COOKER

Roast Pork with Brussels Sprouts and Sweet Potatoes

SERVES 8 - HANDS-ON: 20 MINUTES
UNDER PRESSURE: 36 MINUTES

- **2½ pounds boneless pork shoulder (Boston butt), trimmed and cut into 4 pieces**
- **1 teaspoon paprika**
- **¾ teaspoon salt**
- **⅝ teaspoon freshly ground black pepper**
- **1 garlic clove, minced**
- **1 tablespoon canola oil**
- **1 large onion, cut into 8 wedges**
- **2 cups water**
- **2 tablespoons chopped fresh tarragon**
- **1½ pounds peeled sweet potatoes, cut into 2-inch pieces**
- **1 pound Brussels sprouts, trimmed and halved**
- **½ cup honey mustard**

1. Pat pork dry with paper towels. Combine paprika, ½ teaspoon of the salt, ½ teaspoon of the pepper, and garlic in a small bowl. Sprinkle pork with spice mixture. Remove lid from a 6-quart Instant Pot®. Press [Sauté], and use [Adjust] to select "More" mode. When the word "Hot" appears, swirl in 2 teaspoons of the oil. Add pork to cooker; cook 8 minutes, browning on all sides. Remove pork from cooker.

2. Heat remaining oil in cooker; add onion, and cook, stirring constantly, 3 minutes or until lightly browned. Stir in 2 cups water, scraping inner pot to loosen browned bits. Place pork on top of onion; stir in tarragon. Turn cooker off.

3. Close and lock the lid of the Instant Pot®. Turn the steam release handle to "Sealing" position. Press [Manual]; select "High Pressure," and use [-] or [+] to choose 32 minutes pressure cooking time. When time is up, turn cooker off. Open the cooker using Quick Pressure Release (page 4). Remove pork, and set aside.

4. Add sweet potato and Brussels sprouts to onion mixture in cooker. Close and lock the lid of the Instant Pot®. Turn the steam release handle to "Sealing" position. Press [Manual]; select "High Pressure," and use [-] or [+] to choose 4 minutes pressure cooking time. When time is up, turn cooker off. Open the cooker using Quick Pressure Release (page 4).

5. Remove vegetables with a slotted spoon; place on a serving platter, and sprinkle with remaining ¼ teaspoon salt. Do not toss.

6. Shred pork into bite-sized pieces; place on platter with vegetables. Sprinkle pork with remaining ⅛ teaspoon pepper. Serve pork and vegetables with honey mustard.

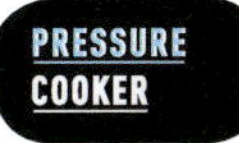

PRESSURE COOKER

Cumin Pork and Poblano Corn

SERVES 6 - HANDS-ON: 25 MINUTES
UNDER PRESSURE: 40 MINUTES

- **1 (2½-pound) bone-in pork shoulder, trimmed**
- **1½ tablespoons chili powder**
- **2 teaspoons ground cumin**
- **½ teaspoon salt**
- **¾ teaspoon freshly ground black pepper**
- **2 tablespoons extra-virgin olive oil**
- **1½ cups water**
- **1½ cups fat-free, lower-sodium chicken broth**
- **1 tablespoon minced fresh garlic**
- **4 poblano chiles, seeded and chopped (about 3 cups)**
- **1 large red bell pepper, diced (about 1½ cups)**
- **4 cups fresh corn kernels (about 5 ears)**
- **¾ cup chopped fresh cilantro**
- **Lime wedges**

1. Pat pork dry with paper towels. Combine chili powder, cumin, ¼ teaspoon of the salt, and black pepper in a medium bowl. Remove 1 tablespoon spice mixture; set aside. Add pork to remaining spice mixture in bowl, turning to coat.

2. Remove lid from a 6-quart Instant Pot®. Press [Sauté]; use [Adjust] to select "More" mode. When the word "Hot" appears, swirl in 1 tablespoon of the oil. Add pork to inner pot; cook 4 minutes, browning on all sides. Remove pork from cooker; add 1½ cups water and the broth, scraping pot to loosen browned bits. Return pork to cooker. Turn cooker off.

3. Close and lock the lid of the Instant Pot®. Turn the steam release handle to "Sealing" position. Press [Manual]; select "High Pressure," and use [-] or [+] to choose 40 minutes pressure cooking time. When time is up, turn cooker off. Open the cooker using Natural Pressure Release (page 4). Remove pork from cooker; separate pork into bite-sized pieces.

4. Strain cooking liquid through a fine sieve into a bowl; discard solids. Skim fat off cooking liquid; discard fat. Return skimmed liquid to cooker. With lid off, press [Sauté], and use [Adjust] to select "More." When mixture comes to a boil, cook until reduced to 2 cups (about 3 to 4 minutes). Pour sauce into a bowl; cover and keep warm.

5. Turn cooker off. Remove inner pot from cooker; wash and dry thoroughly. Return inner pot to cooker. Add remaining 1 tablespoon oil to pot. With lid off, press [Sauté], and use [Adjust] to select "Normal" mode. When oil is hot, swirl to coat the bottom of inner pot. Add reserved 1 tablespoon spice mixture, garlic, poblano chile, and bell pepper. Cook, stirring constantly, 5 minutes or until crisp-tender. Stir in corn, and cook 4 minutes or until thoroughly heated. Turn cooker off. Stir in remaining ¼ teaspoon salt and cilantro. Divide vegetable mixture among 6 plates. Top with pork and sauce; serve with lime wedges.

PRESSURE COOKER

Jambalaya

SERVES 8 - HANDS-ON: 15 MINUTES
UNDER PRESSURE: 18 MINUTES

Andouille, a spiced, heavily smoked sausage, is the signature ingredient in this classic Creole dish.

- **1 teaspoon canola oil**
- **1½ cups (⅛-inch-thick) slices andouille sausage (8 ounces)**
- **1 pound bone-in chicken breast halves, skinned**
- **2½ cups water**
- **1¼ cups uncooked long-grain brown rice**
- **1 cup chopped onion**
- **1 cup chopped red bell pepper**
- **1 cup chopped green bell pepper**
- **1 cup sliced celery**
- **1 teaspoon dried thyme**
- **¼ teaspoon ground red pepper**
- **3 bay leaves**
- **2 teaspoons Old Bay seasoning**
- **1 pound jumbo shrimp, peeled and deveined**
- **1 (14.5-ounce) can diced tomatoes with green pepper, celery, and onion, drained**
- **Sliced scallions (optional)**

1. Remove lid from a 6-quart Instant Pot®. Press [Sauté], and use [Adjust] to select "More" mode. When the word "Hot" appears, swirl in oil. Add sausage; cook 4 minutes or until browned, stirring frequently. Remove sausage from cooker. Add chicken to drippings in cooker; cook 2 minutes on each side or until lightly browned.

2. Stir in 2½ cups water and next 8 ingredients (through bay leaves). Close and lock the lid of the Instant Pot®. Turn the steam release handle to "Sealing" position. Press [Manual]; select "High Pressure," and use [-] or [+] to choose 18 minutes pressure cooking time. When time is up, turn cooker off. Open the cooker using Quick Pressure Release (page 4).

3. Stir in sausage, Old Bay seasoning, shrimp, and tomatoes. With lid off, press [Sauté], and use [Adjust] to select "More" mode. When mixture comes to a boil, turn cooker off. Press [Sauté], and use [Adjust] to select "Normal" mode. Simmer 5 minutes or until shrimp are done, stirring frequently. Turn cooker off. Remove inner pot from cooker; let stand 15 minutes before serving. Divide jambalaya among 8 bowls. Garnish with sliced scallions, if desired.

SWAP IN A SNAP!
Use smoked ham or chorizo if you can't find andouille.

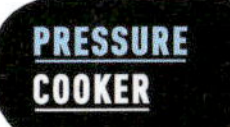

Jalapeño-Glazed Pork Chops and Rice

SERVES 6 - HANDS-ON: 25 MINUTES
UNDER PRESSURE: 23 MINUTES

Jalapeño jelly makes a quick glaze for any type of meat. Add chopped tomatoes to the rice for a balanced meal.

- **6 (8-ounce) bone-in pork chops (about ¾ inch thick)**
- **½ teaspoon salt**
- **½ teaspoon freshly ground black pepper**
- **1 tablespoon canola oil**
- **2 cups uncooked brown basmati rice**
- **1 cup chopped onion**
- **2 garlic cloves, chopped**
- **2½ cups water**
- **2 cups fat-free, lower-sodium chicken broth**
- **½ cup jalapeño pepper jelly**
- **¼ cup sliced scallions**

1. Sprinkle pork chops with ¼ teaspoon of the salt and ¼ teaspoon of the pepper. Remove lid from a 6-quart Instant Pot®. Press [Sauté]; use [Adjust] to select "Normal" mode. When the word "Hot" appears, swirl in 1 teaspoon of the oil. Add 2 pork chops to cooker; cook 2 minutes on each side or until browned. Remove pork from cooker; set aside. Repeat procedure twice with remaining pork chops. Add the remaining 2 teaspoons oil to pot. Add rice, onion, and garlic; cook, stirring constantly, 5 minutes or until onion is tender. Stir in remaining ¼ teaspoon salt, remaining ¼ teaspoon pepper, 2½ cups water, and broth.

2. Close and lock the lid of the Instant Pot®. Turn the steam release handle to "Sealing" position. Press [Manual]; select "High Pressure," and use [-] or [+] to choose 19 minutes pressure cooking time. When time is up, turn cooker off. Open the cooker using Quick Pressure Release (page 4).

3. Add pork chops to cooker. Close and lock the lid of the Instant Pot®. Turn the steam release handle to "Sealing" position. Press [Manual]; select "High Pressure," and use [-] or [+] to choose 4 minutes pressure cooking time. When time is up, turn cooker off. Open the cooker using Quick Pressure Release (page 4).

4. Remove pork chops from cooker. Place rice mixture on a serving platter; top with pork chops. Place jelly in a small microwave-safe bowl. Microwave at HIGH 30 to 60 seconds or until jelly melts. Brush pork chops with warm jelly, and sprinkle with scallions.

Not-Quite-Classic Bolognese

SERVES 8 - HANDS-ON: 25 MINUTES
SLOW COOK: 8 HOURS

Olive oil–flavored cooking spray
1 pound ground sirloin
1 pound lean ground turkey
1 tablespoon olive oil
1 cup diced onion
1 cup diced carrot
¾ cup diced celery
3 garlic cloves, minced
⅓ cup dry white wine
1 teaspoon salt
¾ teaspoon freshly ground black pepper
½ teaspoon dried thyme
¼ teaspoon grated whole nutmeg
1 (28-ounce) can crushed San Marzano tomatoes, undrained
1 bay leaf
16 ounces uncooked spaghetti
¼ cup half-and-half
2 ounces grated fresh Parmigiano-Reggiano cheese (about ½ cup)

1. Coat a large cast-iron skillet with cooking spray. Add beef and turkey to skillet; cook over medium-high heat 7 minutes or until browned, stirring to crumble. Drain well.

2. Remove lid from a 6-quart Instant Pot®. Press [Sauté]; use [Adjust] to select "More" mode. When the word "Hot" appears, swirl in oil. Add onion, carrot, and celery to pot; cook, stirring constantly, 6 minutes or until onions are translucent. Add garlic; cook, stirring constantly, 1 minute. Turn cooker off.

3. Stir in meat mixture, wine, and next 6 ingredients (through bay leaf). Close and lock the lid of the Instant Pot®. Turn the steam release handle to "Venting" position. Press [Slow Cook], and use [Adjust] to select "Less" mode. Press [-] or [+] to choose 8 hours cook time.

4. During last 15 minutes of cooking, cook pasta according to package directions, omitting salt and fat; drain. Remove lid of Instant Pot®, and stir half-and-half into sauce in cooker. Spoon sauce over cooked pasta, and sprinkle with cheese.

Tangy Italian Beef Sandwiches

SERVES 8 - HANDS-ON: 15 MINUTES
SLOW COOK: 8 HOURS

Slow cooking is at its best with this recipe. The beef slowly braises until it practically falls to shreds. Although great on sandwiches, it's also delicious over a baked potato topped with sour cream.

- **3 banana peppers**
- **Cooking spray**
- **2¼ pounds chuck roast, trimmed and halved**
- **½ cup white vinegar**
- **1 tablespoon onion powder**
- **1 tablespoon garlic powder**
- **1½ teaspoons crushed red pepper**
- **½ teaspoon kosher salt**
- **½ teaspoon freshly ground black pepper**
- **7 bottled pepperoncini peppers, chopped**
- **8 hamburger buns, toasted**

1. Preheat broiler.

2. Arrange peppers on a baking sheet coated with cooking spray. Broil 6 minutes or until blackened in spots, turning occasionally.

3. Remove lid from a 6-quart Instant Pot®. Press [Sauté]; use [Adjust] to select "More" mode. When the word "Hot" appears, coat inner pot with cooking spray. Add beef; cook 5 minutes, turning to brown on all sides. Remove beef from pot.

4. Add peppers to pot; stir in vinegar and next 3 ingredients (through crushed red pepper). Stir in ¼ teaspoon of the salt, black pepper, and chopped pepperoncini. Return beef to pot.

5. Close and lock the lid of the Instant Pot®. Turn the steam release handle to "Venting" position. Press [Slow Cook], and use [Adjust] to select "Less" mode. Press [-] or [+] to choose 8 hours cook time.

6. When time is up, remove beef from cooker; shred with 2 forks. Stir beef and remaining ¼ teaspoon salt into cooking liquid. Divide beef mixture evenly among hamburger buns, using a slotted spoon. Serve any extra sauce for dipping.

SWAP IN A SNAP!
Use gluten-free hamburger buns to make this a gluten-free sandwich.

Marinated Flank Steak with Cranberry-Raspberry Salsa

SERVES 16 · HANDS-ON: 10 MINUTES
SLOW COOK: 10 HOURS

This recipe saves a step—it marinates during the cooking, creating a flavorful, tender steak.

- **5 tablespoons fresh lime juice (about 3 limes)**
- **¼ cup bottled chili sauce**
- **3 drops hot pepper sauce (such as Tabasco)**
- **1 (1.25-ounce) package low-sodium taco seasoning**
- **1 (2-pound) flank steak, trimmed**
- **¾ cup (2-inch) sliced scallions**
- **½ cup cilantro sprigs**
- **1 tablespoon chopped seeded jalapeño pepper**
- **1 teaspoon ground cumin**
- **1 (12-ounce) carton cranberry-raspberry crushed fruit**
- **Fresh cilantro (optional)**
- **16 (8-inch) tortillas**

1. Combine ¼ cup of the lime juice and next 3 ingredients (through seasoning) in the inner pot of a 6-quart Instant Pot®. Add steak to pot, turning to coat. Close and lock the lid of the Instant Pot®. Turn the steam release handle to "Venting" position. Press [Slow Cook], and use [Adjust] to select "More" mode. Press [-] or [+] to choose 1 hour cook time. When time is up, turn cooker off, and repeat programing procedure using [Adjust] to select "Less" mode. Press [-] or [+] to choose 9 hours cook time.

2. While steak cooks, place scallions, cilantro sprigs, and jalapeño pepper in a food processor; pulse 5 times or until finely chopped. Add remaining 1 tablespoon lime juice, cumin, and cranberry-raspberry crushed fruit; process until smooth. Spoon mixture into a bowl; cover and chill.

3. When slow cook time is up, remove steak from cooker; discard cooking liquid. Shred steak into bite-sized pieces, and garnish with cilantro, if desired. Warm tortillas according to package directions. Spread about 1½ tablespoons salsa over each tortilla. Spoon about ½ cup shredded steak down center of each tortilla; roll up.

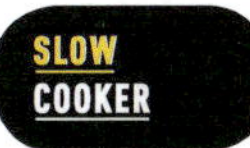

Chili Pepper-Spiked Meat Loaf

SERVES 6 - HANDS-ON: 13 MINUTES
SLOW COOK: 6 HOURS

Chili powder, poblano chiles, and a spicy tomato sauce give everyday meat loaf a makeover. Use two spatulas when removing the meat loaf from the slow cooker.

MEAT LOAF:

- **1 teaspoon olive oil**
- **1¼ cups chopped Vidalia or other sweet onion**
- **1 cup chopped poblano chile**
- **1 teaspoon minced fresh garlic**
- **¾ cup old-fashioned rolled oats**
- **⅓ cup chopped fresh cilantro**
- **1 tablespoon cornstarch**
- **1 tablespoon chili powder**
- **1 teaspoon kosher salt**
- **1 teaspoon ground cumin**
- **1 teaspoon ground coriander**
- **1 teaspoon dried oregano**
- **⅛ teaspoon ground cinnamon**
- **1 pound 93% lean ground beef**
- **1 large egg, lightly beaten**
- **Oregano leaves (optional)**
- **Chopped fresh chives (optional)**

CHILI SAUCE:

- **1 tablespoon cornstarch**
- **1 tablespoon brown sugar**
- **1 tablespoon chili powder**
- **1 (10-ounce) can diced tomatoes and green chiles, undrained**
- **1 (8-ounce) can unsalted tomato sauce**
- **1 chipotle chile, canned in adobo sauce**

1. Make the meat loaf: Heat a large nonstick skillet over medium-high heat. Add oil to pan; swirl to coat. Add onion and chile; cook, stirring constantly, 4 minutes or until onion is tender. Add garlic; cook, stirring constantly, 1 minute. Cool slightly.

2. Combine onion mixture, oats, and next 10 ingredients (through egg). Shape meat mixture into a 7 x 4½-inch loaf. Place in the inner pot of a 6-quart Instant Pot®.

3. Make the chili sauce: Combine all ingredients in a blender; process until smooth. Pour sauce over meat loaf in cooker. Close and lock the lid of the Instant Pot®. Turn the steam release handle to "Venting" position. Press [Slow Cook], and use [Adjust] to select "Less" mode. Press [-] or [+] to choose 6 hours cook time. Serve garnished with oregano leaves and chives, if desired.

Curried Beef Short Ribs

SERVES 6 · HANDS-ON: 15 MINUTES
SLOW COOK: 6 HOURS

- **2 teaspoons canola oil**
- **2 pounds bone-in beef short ribs, trimmed**
- **½ teaspoon kosher salt**
- **¼ teaspoon freshly ground black pepper**
- **⅓ cup minced shallots**
- **3 tablespoons minced fresh garlic**
- **3 tablespoons minced peeled fresh ginger**
- **¼ cup water**
- **2 tablespoons red curry paste**
- **¼ cup light coconut milk**
- **1 tablespoon sugar**
- **1 tablespoon fish sauce**
- **1 teaspoon grated lime rind**
- **1 tablespoon fresh lime juice**
- **4 cups hot cooked basmati rice**
- **Chopped fresh cilantro (optional)**

1. Heat a large nonstick skillet over medium-high heat. Add oil to pan; swirl to coat. Sprinkle ribs with ¼ teaspoon salt and ⅛ teaspoon pepper. Add half of ribs to pan; cook 2 minutes on each side or until browned. Transfer ribs to inner pot of a 6-quart Instant Pot®. Repeat procedure with remaining ribs.

2. Add shallots, garlic, and ginger to pan; sauté 2 minutes. Stir in ¼ cup water and curry paste; cook 1 minute. Stir in coconut milk, sugar, and fish sauce. Add coconut milk mixture to cooker. Close and lock the lid of the Instant Pot®. Turn the steam release handle to "Venting" position. Press [Slow Cook], and use [Adjust] to select "Less" mode. Press [-] or [+] to choose 6 hours cook time.

3. Remove ribs from cooker; keep warm. Strain cooking liquid through a colander over a bowl; discard solids. Skim fat from surface of cooking liquid. Stir ¼ teaspoon salt, ⅛ teaspoon pepper, lime rind, and lime juice into cooking liquid. Shred rib meat with 2 forks; discard bones. Serve rib meat and sauce over cooked rice. Garnish with cilantro, if desired.

Easy Osso Buco

SERVES 6 - HANDS-ON: 10 MINUTES
SLOW COOK: 4 HOURS

Serve over saffron risotto or just plain rice or polenta. Place the veal shanks on their sides so that the meat can fit in the Instant Pot® in a single layer.

- **1 cup finely chopped onion**
- **½ cup finely chopped carrot**
- **½ cup finely chopped celery**
- **¼ cup fat-free, lower-sodium chicken broth**
- **1 tablespoon chopped fresh rosemary**
- **2 teaspoons chopped fresh thyme**
- **1 (14.5-ounce) can whole San Marzano tomatoes, drained and chopped**
- **4 garlic cloves, minced**
- **¾ teaspoon salt**
- **½ teaspoon freshly ground black pepper**
- **4 teaspoons olive oil**
- **6 (10-ounce) veal shanks (2 inches thick)**
- **¾ cup chardonnay or other dry white wine**
- **¼ cup finely chopped fresh parsley**
- **1 teaspoon grated orange rind**
- **1 small garlic clove, minced**

1. Combine first 8 ingredients (through garlic), ¼ teaspoon of the salt, and ¼ teaspoon of the pepper in the inner pot of a 6-quart Instant Pot®.

2. Heat a large nonstick skillet over medium-high heat. Add 2 teaspoons of the oil to pan; swirl to coat. Sprinkle veal with remaining ½ teaspoon salt and remaining ¼ teaspoon pepper. Add half of veal to pan; cook 10 minutes, browning on all sides. Place veal in cooker. Repeat procedure with remaining 2 teaspoons oil and remaining veal. Add wine to pan, scraping pan to loosen browned bits. Bring to a simmer; cook until reduced to ½ cup (about 2 minutes). Pour wine mixture over veal in cooker. Close and lock the lid of the Instant Pot®. Turn the steam release handle to "Venting" position. Press [Slow Cook], and use [Adjust] to select "Less" mode. Press [-] or [+] to choose 4 hours cook time. (Cook additional time, if necessary, until veal is very tender.)

3. Remove veal from cooker; keep warm. Skim fat from surface of cooking liquid; pour cooking liquid into a medium saucepan. Bring to a boil over medium-high heat; cook until reduced to 3 cups (about 13 minutes), stirring occasionally.

4. Combine parsley, orange rind, and 1 garlic clove in a small bowl. Divide veal among 6 shallow bowls; top evenly with cooking liquid and parsley mixture.

Braised Pork Loin with Dried Plums

SERVES 10 - HANDS-ON: 25 MINUTES
SLOW COOK: 6 HOURS

Soaked in savory flavors, the tender meat qualifies as true comfort food.

- **1 (3¼-pound) boneless pork loin roast, trimmed**
- **1½ teaspoons freshly ground black pepper**
- **1 teaspoon salt**
- **1 teaspoon dry mustard**
- **1 teaspoon dried sage**
- **½ teaspoon dried thyme**
- **1 tablespoon olive oil**
- **2 cups sliced onion**
- **1 cup finely chopped leek**
- **1 cup finely chopped carrot**
- **½ cup port or other sweet red wine**
- **⅓ cup fat-free, lower-sodium chicken broth**
- **⅓ cup water**
- **1 cup pitted dried plums (about 20 dried plums)**
- **2 bay leaves**
- **2 tablespoons cornstarch**
- **2 tablespoons water**
- **Thyme leaves (optional)**

1. Cut pork in half crosswise. Combine pepper and next 4 ingredients (through thyme). Rub seasoning mixture over surface of pork halves.

2. Heat a large Dutch oven over medium-high heat. Add oil to pan; swirl to coat. Add pork to pan; cook 5 minutes, browning on all sides. Transfer pork to the inner pot of a 6-quart Instant Pot®. Add onion, leek, and carrot to pan; cook, stirring constantly, 5 minutes or until vegetables are golden. Stir in wine, broth, and ⅓ cup water, scraping pan to loosen browned bits. Pour onion mixture over pork in cooker; add plums and bay leaves.

3. Close and lock the lid of the Instant Pot®. Turn the steam release handle to "Venting" position. Press [Slow Cook], and use [Adjust] to select "More" mode. Press [-] or [+] to choose 1 hour cook time. When time is up, turn cooker off. Press [Slow Cook], and use [Adjust] to select "Less" mode. Press [-] or [+] to choose 5 hours cook time. (Cook additional time, if necessary, until pork is tender.)

4. Remove pork from cooker; keep warm. Combine cornstarch and 2 tablespoons water in a small bowl; stir well. Add cornstarch mixture to cooking liquid in cooker. Turn cooker off.

5. Press [Sauté], and use [Adjust] to select "More" mode. Bring mixture to a boil, and cook 15 minutes or until sauce is thick, stirring frequently. Discard bay leaves. Slice pork, and serve with sauce. Garnish with thyme leaves, if desired.

SLOW COOKER

Pork Loin with Ginger, Fennel, and Apples

SERVES 8 - HANDS-ON: 30 MINUTES
SLOW COOK: 2 HOURS 30 MINUTES

Serve this flavorful dish over polenta.

- **1 (3-pound) boneless pork loin, trimmed**
- **1 teaspoon salt**
- **½ teaspoon freshly ground black pepper**
- **1 tablespoon olive oil**
- **1 fennel bulb (about 8 ounces), thinly sliced**
- **1 red onion, thinly sliced**
- **1 tablespoon minced peeled fresh ginger**
- **2 large garlic cloves, minced**
- **2 small Gala apples (about 12 ounces), cut into ¾-inch-thick slices**
- **2 tablespoons Dijon mustard**
- **2 tablespoons fresh lemon juice**
- **1 teaspoon chopped fresh thyme**
- **1 teaspoon chopped fresh sage**
- **1 (12-ounce) bottle ginger beer**
- **1 tablespoon cornstarch**
- **2 tablespoons water**
- **Thyme leaves (optional)**

1. Sprinkle pork with ½ teaspoon of the salt and ¼ teaspoon of the pepper. Remove lid from a 6-quart Instant Pot®. Press [Sauté]; use [Adjust] to select "More" mode. When the word "Hot" appears, swirl in oil. Add pork to inner pot; cook 10 minutes, browning on all sides. Remove pork from cooker.

2. Add fennel and onion to drippings in pot; cook, stirring constantly, 6 minutes or until lightly browned. Add ginger and garlic; cook, stirring constantly, 1 minute. Stir in apple. Add mustard, next 4 ingredients (through ginger beer), remaining ½ teaspoon salt, and remaining ¼ teaspoon pepper, stirring gently. Nestle pork in center of vegetable mixture. Turn cooker off.

3. Close and lock the lid of the Instant Pot®. Turn the steam release handle to "Venting" position. Press [Slow Cook], and use [Adjust] to select "Less" mode. Press [-] or [+] to choose 2 hours 30 minutes cook time. When time is up, an instant-read thermometer inserted in center of pork should register 145°F. (Cook additional time, if necessary.) Remove lid, leaving cooker in automatic warming mode. Remove pork from cooker; place on a cutting board or work surface, and let stand 15 minutes.

4. While pork stands, strain vegetable mixture through a sieve into a medium saucepan. Return vegetables to inner pot. Combine cornstarch and 2 tablespoons water in a small bowl; add cornstarch mixture to cooking liquid in saucepan. Bring to a boil over medium-high heat, stirring constantly; cook, stirring constantly, 1 minute or until thickened. Cut pork into thin slices; serve pork with vegetable mixture and sauce. Garnish with thyme leaves, if desired.

CHAPTER 4

POULTRY

Chicken with Rich Lemon-Herb Sauce

SERVES 4 - HANDS-ON: 15 MINUTES
UNDER PRESSURE: 25 MINUTES

The secret's definitely in the sauce...so is the flavor. Don't skip the last step—it brings it all together.

- **2 teaspoons chopped fresh thyme**
- **2 teaspoons paprika**
- **1 teaspoon chopped fresh dill**
- **1 teaspoon salt**
- **½ teaspoon freshly ground black pepper**
- **1 pound red potatoes (about 12), cut into 1-inch pieces**
- **8 ounces green beans, trimmed and cut into 2-inch pieces**
- **1 small onion, cut into 8 wedges**
- **2 tablespoons minced fresh garlic**
- **1 tablespoon olive oil**
- **1 (3½-pound) roasting chicken, skinned**
- **1 cup water**
- **3 tablespoons fresh lemon juice**
- **1 tablespoon all-purpose flour**
- **1 tablespoon cold water**

1. Combine first 5 ingredients (through pepper) in a small bowl. Combine potatoes, green beans, onion, and 1 tablespoon of the garlic in a large bowl. Drizzle with oil and sprinkle with 2½ teaspoons spice mixture, tossing to coat.

2. Remove and discard giblets and neck from chicken. Trim excess fat. Sprinkle chicken with remaining spice mixture; rub with remaining 1 tablespoon garlic.

3. Pour 1 cup water into a 6-quart Instant Pot®. Add potato mixture; place chicken on top of potato mixture. Drizzle lemon juice over chicken.

4. Close and lock the lid of the Instant Pot®. Turn the steam release handle to "Sealing" position. Press [Manual]; select "High Pressure," and use [-] or [+] to choose 25 minutes pressure cooking time. When time is up, turn cooker off. Open the cooker using Natural Pressure Release (page 4).

5. Carefully remove chicken with 2 large spoons; place chicken on a platter. Remove vegetables with a slotted spoon, and place around chicken on platter. Skim fat from surface of cooking liquid; discard. Combine flour and 1 tablespoon cold water, stirring with a whisk. Press [Sauté], and use [Adjust] to select "More" mode. Add flour mixture to cooking liquid, stirring with a whisk. When liquid comes to a boil, turn cooker off. Press [Sauté], and use [Adjust] to select "Normal" mode. Simmer 5 minutes or until slightly thick, stirring occasionally. Serve chicken and vegetables with sauce.

PRESSURE COOKER

Chicken with Honey-Lemon Leeks

SERVES 4 - HANDS-ON: 20 MINUTES
UNDER PRESSURE: 11 MINUTES

Lemon is a bright partner for the caramelized leeks and melds beautifully with the honey.

- **8 bone-in, skinless chicken thighs (about 2 pounds)**
- **¾ teaspoon kosher salt**
- **½ teaspoon freshly ground black pepper**
- **1 tablespoon grated lemon rind**
- **4 teaspoons olive oil**
- **4 cups thinly sliced leek (about 3 large)**
- **3 tablespoons fresh lemon juice**
- **2 teaspoons honey**
- **2 tablespoons chopped fresh parsley or chives (optional)**
- **Lemon wedges (optional)**

1. Sprinkle chicken evenly with ½ teaspoon of the salt and pepper. Massage lemon rind into chicken. Remove lid from a 6-quart Instant Pot®. Press [Sauté], and use [Adjust] to select "More" mode. When the word "Hot" appears, swirl in 2 teaspoons of the oil. Add chicken to cooker. Turn cooker off.

2. Close and lock the lid of the Instant Pot®. Turn the steam release handle to "Sealing" position. Press [Manual]; select "High Pressure," and use [-] or [+] to choose 11 minutes pressure cooking time. When time is up, turn cooker off. Open the cooker using Quick Pressure Release (page 4). Remove chicken from cooker, and place on a platter; keep warm.

3. Press [Sauté], and use [Adjust] to select "More" mode. Add remaining 2 teaspoons oil to cooker; swirl to coat. Add leek and remaining ¼ teaspoon salt; cook 15 minutes or until leek begins to brown, scraping inner pot frequently to loosen browned bits. Turn cooker off. Remove inner pot from cooker; stir in lemon juice and honey. Top chicken with leek mixture. If desired, sprinkle with fresh parsley or chives, and serve with lemon wedges.

PRESSURE-PERFECT TIP
Select chicken thighs that are equal in size so they will cook evenly.

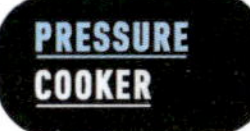

Edamame, Chicken, and Rice Salad

SERVES 8 - HANDS-ON: 9 MINUTES
UNDER PRESSURE: 8 MINUTES

Cooking the chicken in a single layer allows the chicken to brown and not stew. The browned bits left behind help to season the rice.

- **2 tablespoons canola oil**
- **1 pound skinless, boneless chicken breast, cut into bite-sized pieces**
- **1 cup uncooked long-grain brown rice**
- **5 cups water**
- **¾ cup diced red onion**
- **3 cups small broccoli florets**
- **1½ cups diced red bell pepper**
- **1 cup chopped peanuts, toasted**
- **½ cup frozen shelled edamame, thawed**
- **⅓ cup lower-sodium soy sauce**
- **⅓ cup rice vinegar**
- **¼ cup chopped fresh cilantro**
- **1½ tablespoons sugar**
- **1 tablespoon grated peeled fresh ginger**
- **½ teaspoon salt**

1. Remove lid from a 6-quart Instant Pot®. Press [Sauté], and use [Adjust] to select "More" mode. When the word "Hot" appears, swirl in 1 tablespoon of the oil. Add chicken to cooker in a single layer, and cook 2 minutes; stir and cook 4 minutes or until done. Remove chicken from cooker; set aside.

2. Add remaining 1 tablespoon oil, rice, and 5 cups water to cooker, scraping cooker to loosen browned bits. Turn cooker off.

3. Close and lock the lid of the Instant Pot®. Turn the steam release handle to "Sealing" position. Press [Manual]; select "High Pressure," and use [-] or [+] to choose 8 minutes pressure cooking time. When time is up, turn cooker off. Open the cooker using Quick Pressure Release (page 4). While rice mixture cooks, place onion in a medium bowl. Add cold water to cover; let stand 10 minutes. Drain.

4. After pressure is released, stir broccoli into rice mixture in cooker; let stand 30 seconds. Drain broccoli mixture through a fine sieve; rinse with cold water, and drain well.

5. Place broccoli mixture in a large bowl. Add chicken, onion, bell pepper, and remaining ingredients, tossing gently.

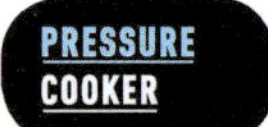

Chicken Fricassee

SERVES 4 - HANDS-ON: 41 MINUTES
UNDER PRESSURE: 11 MINUTES

4 chicken leg quarters (about 2½ pounds), skinned
½ teaspoon kosher salt
½ teaspoon freshly ground black pepper
3 thyme sprigs
2 sage sprigs
1 cup (about 4.5 ounces) all-purpose flour
1 tablespoon olive oil
1 tablespoon butter
1 pound cremini mushrooms, quartered
¾ cup dry white wine
1¼ cups fat-free, lower-sodium chicken broth
1 pound baby carrots
10 ounces pearl onions, peeled
1 tablespoon chopped fresh thyme
1 tablespoon chopped fresh sage

1. Sprinkle chicken with salt and pepper. Tie twine around thyme and sage sprigs. Weigh or lightly spoon flour into a dry measuring cup; level with a knife. Place flour in a shallow dish. Dredge chicken in flour, shaking off excess. Place oil in the inner pot of a 6-quart Instant Pot®; add butter to oil. Press [Sauté], and use [Adjust] to select "Medium" mode. When butter melts, swirl oil mixture to coat bottom of pot. Place 2 chicken leg quarters, flesh sides down, in cooker; cook 5 minutes or until browned. Remove from pot; set aside, and keep warm. Swirl drippings in pot. Add remaining 2 chicken leg quarters. Cook 5 minutes or until browned; remove from pot, and keep warm.

2. Add mushrooms to cooker. Cook, stirring occasionally, 7 minutes or until liquid almost evaporates. Remove mushrooms from cooker using a slotted spoon; set aside, and keep warm.

3. Add wine to cooker; stir, scraping pan with a wooden spoon to loosen browned bits. Bring to a boil; cook 30 seconds. Add chicken, herb sprigs, and broth to cooker. Turn cooker off. Close and lock the lid of the Instant Pot®. Turn the steam release handle to "Sealing" position. Press [Manual]; select "High Pressure," and use [-] or [+] to choose 8 minutes pressure cooking time. When time is up, turn cooker off. Open the cooker using Quick Pressure Release (page 4).

4. Add mushrooms, carrots, and onions to cooker. Close and lock the lid of the Instant Pot®. Turn the steam release handle to "Sealing" position. Press [Manual]; select "High Pressure," and use [-] or [+] to choose 3 minutes pressure cooking time. When time is up, turn cooker off. Open the cooker using Quick Pressure Release (page 4). Remove chicken and vegetables from cooker with a slotted spoon. Arrange chicken and vegetables on a platter; keep warm.

5. Press [Sauté]; use [Adjust] to select "More" mode. Bring to a simmer and cook until cooking liquid is reduced to 1 cup (about 12 minutes), stirring occasionally. Remove herb sprigs; discard. Add chopped thyme and chopped sage to cooking liquid. Serve chicken and vegetables with cooking liquid.

PRESSURE COOKER

Chicken and Sweet Potatoes with Raspberry-Balsamic Reduction

SERVES 4 - HANDS-ON: 15 MINUTES
UNDER PRESSURE: 8 MINUTES

Perfect for any weeknight, these succulent chicken pieces take about 30 minutes to prepare. The sweet and sticky sauce makes this dish taste like you spent all day making it.

2 tablespoons lower-sodium soy sauce
2 tablespoons balsamic vinegar
2 teaspoons Worcestershire sauce
¼ teaspoon salt
¼ teaspoon crushed red pepper
1 tablespoon canola oil
4 chicken drumsticks (about 1 pound), skinned
4 chicken thighs (about 1 pound), skinned
5 shallots, peeled (about 7 ounces)
½ cup water
¼ teaspoon freshly ground black pepper
2 large peeled sweet potatoes (about 1 pound), cut into 2-inch pieces
½ cup raspberry spreadable fruit (such as Smucker's Simply Fruit)
Thyme leaves (optional)

1. Combine first 5 ingredients (through crushed red pepper) in a medium bowl; set aside.

2. Remove lid from a 6-quart Instant Pot®. Press [Sauté], and use [Adjust] to select "More" mode. When the word "Hot" appears, swirl in 1½ teaspoons of the oil. Add half of the chicken to cooker; cook 4 minutes, browning on all sides. Remove chicken from cooker, and keep warm. Repeat procedure with remaining 1½ teaspoons oil and remaining half of chicken. Add shallots to cooker; cook 2 minutes, stirring frequently. Add ½ cup water, scraping cooker to loosen browned bits; stir in black pepper. Turn cooker off. Place chicken on top of shallots; top with sweet potato, and drizzle with 2 tablespoons soy sauce mixture. Do not stir.

3. Close and lock the lid of the Instant Pot®. Turn the steam release handle to "Sealing" position. Press [Manual]; select "High Pressure," and use [-] or [+] to choose 8 minutes pressure cooking time. When time is up, turn cooker off. Open the cooker using Quick Pressure Release (page 4).

4. Remove chicken, potato, and shallots with a slotted spoon, and place on a platter. Add remaining soy sauce mixture and spreadable fruit to cooking liquid in cooker. With lid off, press [Sauté], and use [Adjust] to select "More" mode. When mixture comes to a boil, cook, stirring constantly, until reduced to 1 cup (about 2 minutes). Spoon sauce over chicken, potatoes, and shallots. Sprinkle with thyme, if desired.

PRESSURE COOKER

Spicy Asian Chicken Thighs

SERVES 8 - HANDS-ON: 15 MINUTES
UNDER PRESSURE: 17 MINUTES

Serve these saucy chicken thighs over cooked noodles with a side of steamed broccoli for a well-rounded meal.

- **8 bone-in chicken thighs (about 1¾ pounds), skinned**
- **1 cup water**
- **½ cup hoisin sauce**
- **¼ cup rice vinegar**
- **1 tablespoon brown sugar**
- **2 tablespoons minced peeled fresh ginger**
- **1 tablespoon minced fresh garlic**
- **2 tablespoons sambal oelek (ground fresh chile paste)**
- **2 tablespoons fresh lime juice**
- **1 tablespoon dark sesame oil**
- **Cooking spray**
- **¼ cup thinly sliced scallions**
- **¼ cup cilantro leaves**
- **Lime wedges (optional)**

1. Pat chicken dry with a paper towel. Combine 1 cup water and next 8 ingredients (through sesame oil) in a large bowl. Add chicken, turning to coat. Place chicken mixture in a 6-quart Instant Pot®. Close and lock the lid of the Instant Pot®. Turn the steam release handle to "Sealing" position. Press [Manual]; select "High Pressure," and use [-] or [+] to choose 17 minutes pressure cooking time. When time is up, turn cooker off. Open the cooker using Quick Pressure Release (page 4).

2. While chicken mixture cooks, preheat broiler.

3. Line a jelly-roll pan with foil; coat foil with cooking spray. Remove chicken from cooker with tongs, and place on prepared pan. Broil chicken 3 minutes on each side or until crisp and lightly charred.

4. While chicken broils, press [Sauté] on cooker, and use [Adjust] to select "More" mode. Bring cooking liquid to a boil; cook, uncovered, 5 minutes or until slightly thick.

5. Sprinkle chicken with scallions and cilantro; serve with sauce and, if desired, lime wedges.

PRESSURE-PERFECT TIP
Finish these chicken thighs in the broiler to ensure a crispy outside and a juicy inside.

Chicken, Shrimp, and Vegetable Gumbo

SERVES 8 - HANDS-ON: 20 MINUTES
UNDER PRESSURE: 23 MINUTES

This hearty dish freezes well and tastes even better the next day. Serve in bowls as is or over rice.

- ¼ **cup (about 1.1 ounces) all-purpose flour**
- ¼ **cup canola oil**
- 1½ **cups diced green bell pepper**
- 1 **cup diced onion**
- 1 **cup chopped celery**
- 1 **garlic clove, chopped**
- 3 **cups water**
- 1 **tablespoon Old Bay seasoning**
- 1 **teaspoon garlic powder**
- ½ **teaspoon salt**
- 2 **(14.5-ounce) cans stewed tomatoes, undrained**
- 1½ **pounds skinless, boneless chicken thighs, cut into 1-inch pieces**
- 4 **bay leaves**
- 1 **tablespoon hot sauce**
- 1 **pound okra, cut into 1-inch pieces**
- 1 **pound peeled and deveined medium shrimp**

1. Weigh or lightly spoon flour into a dry measuring cup; level with a knife. With lid off a 6-quart Instant Pot®, press [Sauté], and use [Adjust] to select "Normal" mode. Combine flour and oil in cooker; cook 5 minutes, stirring constantly with a flat spatula until dark brown.

2. Add bell pepper and next 3 ingredients (through garlic); cook 3 minutes, stirring frequently. Stir in 3 cups water and next 6 ingredients (through bay leaves). Turn cooker off.

3. Close and lock the lid of the Instant Pot®. Turn the steam release handle to "Sealing" position. Press [Manual]; select "High Pressure," and use [-] or [+] to choose 23 minutes pressure cooking time. When time is up, turn cooker off. Open the cooker using Natural Pressure Release (page 4).

4. Stir in hot sauce and okra. Press [Sauté], and use [Adjust] to select "More" mode. Cook, uncovered, 5 minutes, stirring occasionally. Add shrimp; cook 5 minutes or until done and okra is tender. Remove and discard bay leaves.

PRESSURE-PERFECT TIP
Cook the shrimp and okra without pressure for the best texture.

SLOW COOKER

Spicy Chicken Cacciatore

SERVES 8 - HANDS-ON: 16 MINUTES
SLOW COOK: 3 HOURS 30 MINUTES

Serve this saucy dish over pasta. Transform any leftovers into soup by shredding the chicken and combining the sauce with chicken stock, diced zucchini, and carrots.

- **½ cup (about 2.2 ounces) all-purpose flour**
- **8 skinless, boneless chicken thighs (about 2 pounds)**
- **1 tablespoon olive oil**
- **2 cups chopped red bell pepper**
- **2 (8-ounce) containers refrigerated prechopped onion (about 3 cups)**
- **6 garlic cloves, minced**
- **½ cup dry red wine**
- **½ cup canned tomato purée**
- **2 tablespoons capers, drained**
- **1½ teaspoons crushed red pepper**
- **1 teaspoon dried oregano**
- **1 teaspoon freshly ground black pepper**
- **¾ teaspoon salt**
- **1 (14.5-ounce) can unsalted diced tomatoes, undrained**
- **¼ cup chopped fresh parsley**

1. Weigh or lightly spoon flour into a dry measuring cup; level with a knife. Place flour in a shallow dish. Dredge chicken in flour, turning to coat; shake off excess flour. Discard any remaining flour.

2. Heat a large skillet over medium-high heat. Add oil to pan; swirl to coat. Add half of chicken; cook 3 to 4 minutes on each side or until browned. Transfer chicken to a 6-quart Instant Pot®. Repeat procedure with remaining chicken.

3. Add bell pepper, onion, and garlic to pan. Cook, stirring constantly, 4 minutes. Stir in wine. Cook 2 minutes, scraping pan to loosen browned bits. Stir in tomato purée. Add chicken, capers, and next 5 ingredients (through tomatoes) to cooker.

4. Close and lock the lid of the Instant Pot®. Turn the steam release handle to "Venting" position. Press [Slow Cook], and use [Adjust] to select "Less" mode. Press [-] or [+] to choose 3 hours 30 minutes cook time. Sprinkle with parsley before serving.

Chicken Paprikash

SERVES 6 - HANDS-ON: 25 MINUTES
SLOW COOK: 3 HOURS

Serve this flavorful slow-cooker chicken over egg noodles, rice, or mashed potaotes. Make sure the mushrooms are submerged in liquid while cooking.

- **6 skinless, boneless chicken thighs (about 1¾ pounds), trimmed**
- **½ teaspoon salt**
- **½ teaspoon freshly ground black pepper**
- **3 tablespoons white rice flour**
- **1 tablespoon canola oil**
- **2 cups chopped onion**
- **1 cup chopped red bell pepper**
- **½ cup matchstick-cut carrots**
- **3 garlic cloves, minced**
- **Cooking spray**
- **1 (8-ounce) package presliced mushrooms**
- **1¼ cups fat-free, lower-sodium chicken broth**
- **2 tablespoons Hungarian sweet paprika**
- **½ cup reduced-fat sour cream**
- **1 tablespoon chopped fresh parsley**

1. Sprinkle chicken with ¼ teaspoon of the salt and ¼ teaspoon of the black pepper. Place flour in a shallow dish; dredge chicken in flour, reserving any remaining flour. Heat a large well-seasoned cast-iron skillet over medium-high heat. Add oil to pan; swirl to coat. Add chicken to pan; cook 3 minutes on each side or until golden brown. Transfer chicken to a 6-quart Instant Pot®.

2. Add onion and next 3 ingredients (through garlic) to pan; coat vegetables with cooking spray. Cook, stirring constantly, 6 minutes or just until tender. Transfer onion mixture to cooker.

3. Coat mushrooms with cooking spray, and add to pan. Cook, stirring constantly, 5 minutes or until browned. Transfer mushrooms to cooker.

4. Combine reserved flour, remaining ¼ teaspoon salt, remaining ¼ teaspoon black pepper, broth, and paprika in a bowl; stir with a whisk. Add broth mixture to cooker. Close and lock the lid of the Instant Pot®. Turn the steam release handle to "Venting" position. Press [Slow Cook], and use [Adjust] to select "Less" mode. Press [-] or [+] to choose 3 hours cook time.

5. Remove chicken from cooker, and place on a serving platter. Skim fat from surface of cooking liquid. Stir sour cream into cooking liquid. Serve sauce with chicken, and sprinkle with parsley.

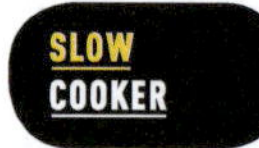

Chicken Korma

SERVES 8 - HANDS-ON: 15 MINUTES
SLOW COOK: 6 HOURS

- **2 pounds skinless, boneless chicken thighs, cut into bite-sized pieces**
- **2 cups coarsely chopped onion (1 onion)**
- **2 tablespoons minced peeled fresh ginger**
- **2 teaspoons curry powder**
- **1 teaspoon ground coriander**
- **½ teaspoon ground cumin**
- **½ teaspoon crushed red pepper**
- **4 garlic cloves, minced**
- **2 cups (½-inch) cubed peeled baking potato**
- **1 teaspoon salt**
- **1 (14.5-ounce) can diced tomatoes, undrained**
- **2 bay leaves**
- **1 (3-inch) cinnamon stick**
- **½ cup plain fat-free yogurt**
- **4 cups hot cooked long-grain brown rice**
- **¼ cup chopped fresh cilantro**

1. Heat a large nonstick skillet over medium-high heat. Add chicken to pan; cook 8 minutes or until lightly browned, turning occasionally. Transfer chicken to a 6-quart Instant Pot®. Add onion to pan; cook, stirring constantly, 3 minutes. Add ginger and next 5 ingredients (through garlic) to pan; cook, stirring constantly, 2 minutes. Pour onion mixture over chicken in cooker. Stir in potato and next 4 ingredients (through cinnamon stick).

2. Close and lock the lid of the Instant Pot®. Turn the steam release handle to "Venting" position. Press [Slow Cook], and use [Adjust] to select "Less" mode. Press [-] or [+] to choose 6 hours cook time. Discard bay leaves and cinnamon stick. Turn cooker off. Let chicken mixture stand 15 minutes. Stir in yogurt. Serve chicken mixture over rice, and sprinkle with cilantro.

Peanut Chicken and Sugar Snap Peas with Noodles

SERVES 6 · HANDS-ON: 11 MINUTES
SLOW COOK: 2 HOURS

1½ pounds chicken breast tenders, cut into bite-sized pieces
3 tablespoons cornstarch
2 tablespoons teriyaki sauce
2 teaspoons minced fresh garlic
¼ teaspoon crushed red pepper
1 teaspoon dark sesame oil
2 cups fat-free, lower-sodium chicken broth
¼ cup natural-style peanut butter
2½ cups trimmed sugar snap peas
1 cup matchstick-cut carrots
1 (12-ounce) package spaghetti
½ cup sliced scallions
¼ cup chopped unsalted, dry-roasted peanuts
Lime wedges (optional)

1. Combine chicken, 2 tablespoons of the cornstarch, 1 tablespoon of the teriyaki sauce, 1 teaspoon of the garlic, and red pepper in a bowl; toss well. Heat a large nonstick skillet over medium-high heat. Add oil to pan; swirl to coat. Add chicken mixture to pan; cook 6 minutes, browning on all sides. Stir in ½ cup of the broth, scraping pan to loosen browned bits. Transfer chicken mixture to the inner pot of a 6-quart Instant Pot®.

2. Combine remaining 1½ cups broth, peanut butter, remaining 1 tablespoon cornstarch, remaining 1 tablespoon teriyaki sauce, and remaining 1 teaspoon garlic in a bowl; pour over chicken mixture.

3. Close and lock the lid of the Instant Pot®. Turn the steam release handle to "Venting" position. Press [Slow Cook], and use [Adjust] to select "More" mode. Press [-] or [+] to choose 1 hour 30 minutes cook time. Stir in peas and carrots; repeat slow cook procedure, choosing 30 minutes cook time. When time is up, peas should be crisp-tender.

4. While peas and carrots cook, cook pasta according to package directions, omitting salt and fat; drain. Add cooked spaghetti to chicken mixture in cooker; toss well. Sprinkle with scallions and peanuts; serve with lime wedges, if desired.

Chicken and Kaffir Lime Curry

SERVES 5 - HANDS-ON: 14 MINUTES
SLOW COOK: 1 HOUR

- **1¼ pounds skinless, boneless chicken breasts, cut into bite-sized pieces**
- **1½ tablespoons cornstarch**
- **2 teaspoons red curry powder**
- **¼ teaspoon salt**
- **1 teaspoon olive oil**
- **2 cups chicken stock (such as Kitchen Basics)**
- **1 (13.66-ounce) can light coconut milk**
- **6 kaffir lime leaves**
- **3 cups water**
- **1½ cups uncooked jasmine rice**
- **Sliced scallions (optional)**
- **Chopped fresh cilantro (optional)**

1. Sprinkle chicken with 1 tablespoon of the cornstarch, 1 teaspoon of the curry powder, and salt. Heat a large nonstick skillet over medium-high heat. Add oil to pan; swirl to coat. Add chicken to pan; cook, stirring constantly, 5 to 6 minutes or until golden brown. Stir in ½ cup of the stock, scraping pan to loosen browned bits. Transfer chicken mixture to inner pot of a 6-quart Instant Pot®.

2. Combine remaining 1½ cups stock, remaining 1½ teaspoons cornstarch, remaining 1 teaspoon curry powder, and coconut milk in a bowl; stir with a whisk. Stir coconut milk mixture into chicken mixture in cooker. Add kaffir lime leaves.

3. Close and lock the lid of the Instant Pot®. Turn the steam release handle to "Venting" position. Press [Slow Cook], and use [Adjust] to select "More" mode. Press [-] or [+] to choose 1 hour cook time. Discard lime leaves.

4. During last 25 minutes of cook time, bring 3 cups water to a boil in a large saucepan; add rice. Cover, reduce heat, and simmer 20 minutes or until liquid is absorbed. Serve chicken mixture over rice; sprinkle with scallions and cilantro, if desired.

Tiny French Beans with Smoked Sausage

SERVES 4 - HANDS-ON: 15 MINUTES
SLOW COOK: 8 HOURS

- **1 pound smoked turkey sausage, cut into 1½-inch pieces**
- **1 tablespoon canola oil**
- **⅓ cup minced shallots**
- **3 garlic cloves, minced**
- **2 cups dried flageolets (about 1 pound)**
- **2 cups water**
- **¼ cup minced fresh or 1 tablespoon dried thyme**
- **1 teaspoon celery seeds**
- **¼ teaspoon freshly ground black pepper**
- **1 (14.5-ounce) can fat-free, lower-sodium chicken broth**
- **Thyme sprigs (optional)**

1. Heat a large nonstick skillet over medium heat. Add sausage to pan; cook, stirring constantly, 5 minutes or until browned. Transfer sausage to the inner pot of a 6-quart Instant Pot®. Heat oil in pan over medium heat. Add shallots and garlic to pan; cook, stirring constantly, 1 minute. Add shallot mixture to pot.

2. Sort and wash beans. Add beans, 2 cups water, and next 4 ingredients (through chicken broth) to pot. Close and lock the lid of the Instant Pot®. Turn the steam release handle to "Venting" position. Press [Slow Cook], and use [Adjust] to select "More" mode. Press [-] or [+] to choose 8 hours cook time. (Cook additional time, if necessary, until beans are tender.) Serve with thyme sprigs, if desired.

CHAPTER 5

MEATLESS

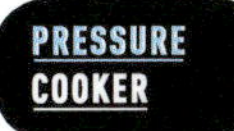

Chickpea Tikka Masala

SERVES 6 - HANDS-ON: 10 MINUTES
UNDER PRESSURE: 40 MINUTES

This delicious meatless recipe is a quick and easy swap for the traditional chicken tikka masala.

- **8 ounces dried chickpeas (garbanzo beans)**
- **2 tablespoons canola oil**
- **1½ cups diced onion**
- **1½ cups diced carrot**
- **1½ teaspoons curry powder**
- **1 teaspoon ground cumin**
- **¼ teaspoon ground red pepper**
- **4 cups water**
- **1 cup frozen petite green peas**
- **½ cup chopped fresh cilantro**
- **1 tablespoon grated peeled fresh ginger**
- **1 teaspoon sugar**
- **¾ teaspoon salt**
- **1 (14.5-ounce) can diced tomatoes, undrained**
- **1 (13.5-ounce) can light coconut milk**
- **¾ cup uncooked whole-wheat couscous**
- **1 lime, cut into 6 wedges**

1. Sort and wash chickpeas; drain. Remove lid from a 6-quart Instant Pot®. Press [Sauté], and then use [Adjust] to select "More" mode. When the word "Hot" appears, swirl in 1 tablespoon of the oil. Add onion; cook, stirring frequently, 4 minutes or until browned. Add remaining 1 tablespoon oil, carrot, and next 3 ingredients (through red pepper); cook 30 seconds, stirring constantly. Add chickpeas and 2¾ cups of the water to cooker. Turn cooker off.

2. Close and lock the lid of cooker. Turn the steam release handle to "Sealing" position. Press [Manual]; select "High Pressure," and use [-] or [+] to choose 40 minutes pressure cooking time. When time is up, turn cooker off. Open the cooker using Natural Pressure Release (page 4). Stir in green peas and next 6 ingredients (through coconut milk). Press [Sauté], and use [Adjust] to select "More" mode. Cook, uncovered, 5 minutes or until thoroughly heated.

3. While chickpeas cook, bring remaining 1¼ cups water to a boil in a medium saucepan. Remove from heat, and stir in couscous. Cover and let stand 5 minutes. Fluff with a fork. Divide couscous among 6 shallow bowls; top with chickpea mixture, and serve with lime wedges.

Lemon, Wheat Berry, and Chickpea Salad

SERVES 10 - HANDS-ON: 10 MINUTES
UNDER PRESSURE: 35 MINUTES

Look for wheat berries in the grain or bulk section of your supermarket.

- **8 ounces dried chickpeas (garbanzo beans)**
- **8 ounces uncooked wheat berries (hard winter wheat)**
- **8 cups water**
- **¼ cup extra-virgin olive oil**
- **1½ cups frozen green peas**
- **1½ cups diced English cucumber**
- **1 cup sliced bottled roasted red bell pepper**
- **¾ cup diced red onion**
- **2 teaspoons grated lemon rind**
- **¼ cup fresh lemon juice**
- **2 teaspoons dried dill**
- **¼ teaspoon freshly ground black pepper**
- **4 ounces crumbled feta cheese (about 1 cup)**
- **1¼ teaspoons salt**

1. Sort and wash chickpeas. Combine chickpeas, wheat berries, 8 cups water, and 1 tablespoon of the oil in a 6-quart Instant Pot®. Close and lock the lid of the Instant Pot®. Turn the steam release handle to "Sealing" position. Press [Manual]; select "High Pressure," and use [-] or [+] to choose 35 minutes pressure cooking time. When time is up, turn cooker off. Open the cooker using Natural Pressure Release (page 4).

2. While cooker stands, combine remaining 3 tablespoons oil, peas, and next 7 ingredients (through black pepper) in a large bowl. Drain chickpea mixture through a fine sieve. Rinse with cold water; drain well. Add chickpea mixture to bowl; toss well. Stir in feta cheese and salt. Serve immediately, or cover and chill.

PRESSURE COOKER

Red Beans and Rice

SERVES 8 - HANDS-ON: 15 MINUTES
UNDER PRESSURE: 25 MINUTES

- **1 pound dried red kidney beans**
- **8 cups water**
- **1 tablespoon olive oil**
- **1 pound andouille sausage, cut into ¾-inch pieces**
- **1½ cups chopped onion**
- **1½ cups chopped poblano chile**
- **1 cup diced celery**
- **2 tablespoons chopped fresh thyme**
- **½ teaspoon kosher salt**
- **10 garlic cloves, crushed**
- **1 (12-ounce) can beer**
- **4 cups unsalted chicken stock**
- **½ teaspoon ground red pepper**
- **¼ teaspoon freshly ground black pepper**
- **3 bay leaves**
- **½ cup thinly sliced scallions**
- **2 tablespoons cider vinegar**
- **4 cups hot cooked long-grain rice**

1. Sort and wash beans; place in a 6-quart Instant Pot®. Add 8 cups water. Close and lock the lid of the Instant Pot®. Turn the steam release handle to "Sealing" position. Press [Manual]; select "High Pressure," and use [-] or [+] to choose 25 minutes pressure cooking time. When time is up, turn cooker off. Open the cooker using Quick Pressure Release (page 4). Drain beans; discard cooking liquid.

2. Wash inner pot, and dry thoroughly. Return inner pot to cooker. Press [Sauté]; use [Adjust] to select "More" mode. When the word "Hot" appears, swirl in oil. Add sausage; cook, stirring frequently, 6 minutes or until browned. Add onion and next 5 ingredients (through garlic); cook 8 minutes. Stir in beer. When mixture comes to a boil, cook 2 minutes, scraping pan to loosen browned bits. Add beans, stock, and next 3 ingredients (through bay leaves). Return to a boil; turn cooker off. Press [Sauté], and use [Adjust] to select "Normal" mode. Simmer 10 minutes. Remove and discard bay leaves. Stir in ¼ cup of the scallions and vinegar. Serve over rice; sprinkle with remaining ¼ cup scallions.

PRESSURE COOKER

Minestrone Soup

SERVES 8 - HANDS-ON: 15 MINUTES
UNDER PRESSURE: 6 MINUTES

This hearty soup is chock-full of antioxidants and fiber from colorful veggies, beans, and dark leafy greens.

- **2 tablespoons olive oil**
- **1 medium onion, chopped (about 1¼ cups)**
- **3 tablespoons minced fresh or 1 tablespoon dried parsley**
- **1 large garlic clove, minced**
- **3 (14.5-ounce) cans fat-free, lower-sodium chicken broth**
- **1 (16-ounce) can pinto beans, undrained**
- **4 medium tomatoes, peeled and coarsely chopped (about 4 cups)**
- **2 medium celery stalks, sliced (about 1 cup)**
- **2 medium carrots, sliced (about 1 cup)**
- **1 medium zucchini, halved lengthwise and sliced (about 2 cups)**
- **½ cup uncooked elbow macaroni**
- **2 teaspoons dried basil, crushed**
- **½ teaspoon salt**
- **½ teaspoon dried Italian seasoning**
- **⅛ teaspoon dried crushed red pepper**
- **5 cups packed coarsely chopped stemmed kale leaves**
- **Freshly grated Parmesan cheese**

1. Remove lid from a 6-quart Instant Pot®. Press [Sauté].

Use [Adjust] to select "Normal" mode. When the word "Hot" appears, swirl in oil. Add onion. Cook, stirring frequently, 5 minutes or until onion is tender but not brown. Add parsley and garlic. Cook, stirring constantly, 30 seconds. Immediately add chicken broth and beans.

2. Stir in tomato and next 8 ingredients (through crushed red pepper). Turn cooker off. Close and lock the lid of the Instant Pot®. Turn the steam release handle to "Sealing" position. Press [Manual]; select "High Pressure," and use [-] or [+] to choose 6 minutes pressure cooking time. When time is up, turn cooker off. Open the cooker using Quick Pressure Release (page 4). Press [Sauté]. Use [Adjust] to select "More" mode.

3. Add kale, stirring frequently, 2 to 3 minutes or until soup just comes to a boil and kale wilts. Turn cooker off.

4. Ladle soup into bowls; sprinkle with Parmesan cheese.

Note: For ease in preparing kale, fold the leaves in half lengthwise. Cut out the ribs, and roll up several leaves together. Cut leaf roll in half lengthwise and then crosswise into 1-inch pieces. Rinse in 3 washings of cold water, draining between washings, and finish with a whirl in a salad spinner to remove sandy grit.

Risotto with Tomato Topping

SERVES 10 - HANDS-ON: 10 MINUTES
UNDER PRESSURE: 7 MINUTES

TOPPING:

- **1½ cups chopped seeded tomato**
- **2 tablespoons chopped scallions**
- **1½ teaspoons extra-virgin olive oil**
- **1 teaspoon balsamic vinegar**
- **¼ teaspoon crushed red pepper**
- **⅛ teaspoon sugar**
- **⅛ teaspoon salt**
- **⅛ teaspoon freshly ground black pepper**

RISOTTO:

- **2 tablespoons butter**
- **1 cup chopped onion**
- **1½ cups Arborio rice or other medium-grain rice**
- **2 garlic cloves, minced**
- **½ cup dry white wine**
- **4 cups fat-free, lower-sodium chicken broth**
- **½ teaspoon salt**
- **¼ teaspoon freshly ground black pepper**
- **⅛ teaspoon ground nutmeg**
- **4 ounces grated fresh Parmesan cheese (about 1 cup)**
- **⅓ cup finely chopped fresh basil**
- **1 teaspoon grated lemon rind**
- **2 tablespoons fresh lemon juice**

1. Make the topping: Combine first 8 ingredients (through black pepper) in a bowl. Cover; let stand at room temperature.

2. Make the risotto: Remove lid from a 6-quart Instant Pot®. Press [Sauté]; use [Adjust] to select "Normal" mode. Add butter, and cook until melted. Add onion; cook, stirring, constantly, 2 minutes. Add rice and garlic; cook, stirring constantly, 2 minutes. Add wine; cook 1 minute or until liquid is absorbed, stirring frequently. Stir in broth and next 3 ingredients (through nutmeg). Turn cooker off.

3. Close and lock the lid of the Instant Pot®. Turn the steam release handle to "Sealing" position. Press [Manual]; select "High Pressure," and use [-] or [+] to choose 7 minutes pressure cooking time. When time is up, turn cooker off. Open the cooker using Natural Pressure Release (page 4). Stir in cheese and next 3 ingredients (through lemon juice). Serve risotto with tomato topping.

PRESSURE-PERFECT TIP
Don't worry if the rice is a tad runny after cooking—it thickens as it stands.

Cheddar-Fontina Penne

SERVES 6 - HANDS-ON: 21 MINUTES
UNDER PRESSURE: 3 MINUTES

For a smooth sauce, be sure to combine the flour and water before adding it to the pot.

- **1 tablespoon plus 1 teaspoon extra-virgin olive oil**
- **½ cup panko (Japanese breadcrumbs)**
- **3¾ cups water**
- **1 (14.5-ounce) package multigrain penne (tube-shaped pasta)**
- **⅔ cup evaporated low-fat milk**
- **¾ teaspoon garlic powder**
- **¾ teaspoon salt**
- **¼ teaspoon freshly ground black pepper**
- **¼ teaspoon ground red pepper**
- **2 teaspoons all-purpose flour**
- **3 ounces sharp white cheddar cheese, shredded (about ¾ cup)**
- **3 ounces fontina cheese, shredded (about ¾ cup)**
- **1 cup grape tomatoes, halved**
- **¼ cup finely chopped scallions**

1. Remove lid from a 6-quart Instant Pot®. Press [Sauté]; use [Adjust] to select "Normal" mode. When the word "Hot" appears, swirl in 1 tablespoon of the oil. Add panko; cook, stirring constantly, 1 minute or until golden brown. Turn cooker off. Remove panko from inner pot; set aside. Wipe inner pot with a paper towel.

2. Add 3½ cups of the water and pasta to cooker. Close and lock the lid of the Instant Pot®. Turn the steam release handle to "Sealing" position. Press [Manual]; select "High Pressure," and use [-] or [+] to choose 3 minutes pressure cooking time. Open the cooker using Quick Pressure Release (page 4).

3. Remove pasta with a slotted spoon; place in a medium bowl. Add milk and next 4 ingredients (through red pepper) to cooking liquid. Combine remaining ¼ cup water and flour in a small bowl; gradually add to milk mixture, stirring with a whisk. With lid off, press [Sauté], and use [Adjust] to select "More" mode. Bring to a boil; cook 5 minutes or until slightly thick. Turn cooker off. Add cheeses, stirring until cheeses melt. Stir in cooked pasta, tossing gently to coat.

4. Heat a medium nonstick skillet over medium-high heat. Add remaining 1 teaspoon oil to pan; swirl to coat. Add tomatoes; sauté 2 minutes or until soft. Top pasta mixture with tomatoes and scallions; sprinkle with panko.

Spinach and Goat Cheese Lasagna

SERVES 8 - HANDS-ON: 15 MINUTES
SLOW COOK: 2 HOURS

Use no-cook lasagna noodles since the time in the slow cooker will bring the noodles to a perfect texture while binding the layers together.

- **1 teaspoon extra-virgin olive oil**
- **1¾ cups chopped onion**
- **1 cup diced zucchini**
- **½ cup shredded carrot**
- **2 garlic cloves, chopped**
- **½ teaspoon salt**
- **½ teaspoon freshly ground black pepper**
- **1 (28-ounce) can crushed tomatoes, undrained**
- **Cooking spray**
- **1 cup chopped fresh basil**
- **¾ cup part-skim ricotta cheese**
- **2 (10-ounce) packages frozen chopped spinach, thawed, drained, and squeezed dry**
- **2 ounces goat cheese (about ¼ cup)**
- **8 (0.75-ounce) gluten-free lasagna noodles**
- **1 ounce shredded fresh Parmesan cheese (about ¼ cup)**
- **Basil leaves (optional)**

1. Heat a 4-quart saucepan over medium heat. Add oil to pan; swirl to coat. Add onion, zucchini, and carrot; cook, stirring constantly, 5 minutes. Add garlic; cook, stirring constantly, 1 minute. Stir in salt, pepper, and tomatoes; bring to a simmer, and cook 5 minutes, stirring occasionally.

2. Coat the inner pot of a 6-quart Instant Pot® with cooking spray. Combine basil and next 3 ingredients (through goat cheese) in a medium bowl. Spread ½ cup spinach mixture in cooker. Arrange one-third of noodles over spinach mixture, breaking noodles as necessary to fit cooker; top with half of remaining spinach mixture and 1 cup tomato mixture. Repeat procedure once, ending with noodles. Pour remaining tomato mixture over noodles, being careful to cover noodles completely.

3. Close and lock the lid of the Instant Pot®. Turn the steam release handle to "Venting" position. Press [Slow Cook], and use [Adjust] to select "Less" mode. Press [-] or [+] to choose 2 hours cook time.

4. Uncover and sprinkle with Parmesan cheese; cover and let stand 15 minutes before serving. Garnish with basil leaves, if desired.

Brown Rice-Stuffed Cabbage Rolls with Pine Nuts and Currants

SERVES 4 - HANDS-ON: 50 MINUTES
SLOW COOK: 2 HOURS

Assemble this dish the night before for a head start on a great next day's dinner.

1 large head green cabbage, cored
1 tablespoon olive oil
1½ cups finely chopped onion
3 cups cooked brown rice
3 ounces crumbled feta cheese (about ¾ cup)
½ cup dried currants
2 tablespoons pine nuts, toasted
2 tablespoons chopped fresh parsley
¼ teaspoon salt
½ teaspoon freshly ground black pepper
½ cup apple juice
1 tablespoon cider vinegar
1 (14.5-ounce) can crushed tomatoes, undrained
Additional chopped fresh parsley (optional)

1. Steam cabbage head 8 minutes; cool slightly. Remove 16 leaves from cabbage head; discard remaining cabbage. Cut off raised portion of the center vein of each cabbage leaf (do not cut out vein); set trimmed cabbage leaves aside.

2. Heat oil in a large nonstick skillet over medium heat; swirl to coat. Add onion; cover and cook 6 minutes or until tender. Remove from heat; stir in brown rice and next 4 ingredients (through parsley). Stir in ¼ teaspoon of the salt and ⅛ teaspoon of the pepper.

3. Place cabbage leaves on a flat surface; spoon about ⅓ cup rice mixture into center of each cabbage leaf. Fold in edges of leaves over rice mixture; roll up. Arrange cabbage rolls in bottom of the inner pot of a 6-quart Instant Pot®.

4. Combine the remaining ¼ teaspoon salt, remaining ⅛ teaspoon pepper, apple juice, vinegar, and tomatoes; pour evenly over cabbage rolls. Close and lock the lid of the Instant Pot®. Turn the steam release handle to "Venting" position. Press [Slow Cook], and use [Adjust] to select "More" mode. Press [-] or [+] to choose 2 hours cook time. Serve sprinkled with parsley, if desired.

SLOW COOKER

Thyme-Scented White Bean Cassoulet

SERVES 6 - HANDS-ON: 15 MINUTES
SLOW COOK: 8 HOURS

Butter-tossed breadcrumbs stirred in at the end give this dish a robust stew-like consistency.

- **1 tablespoon olive oil**
- **1½ cups chopped onion**
- **1½ cups (½-inch-thick) slices diagonally cut carrot**
- **1 cup (½-inch-thick) slices diagonally cut parsnip**
- **2 garlic cloves, minced**
- **3 cups cooked Great Northern beans**
- **¾ cup organic vegetable broth**
- **½ teaspoon dried thyme**
- **¼ teaspoon salt**
- **¼ teaspoon freshly ground black pepper**
- **1 (28-ounce) can diced tomatoes, undrained**
- **1 bay leaf**
- **¼ cup dry breadcrumbs**
- **1 ounce grated fresh Parmesan cheese (about ¼ cup)**
- **2 tablespoons butter, melted**
- **2 links frozen meatless Italian sausage, thawed and chopped**
- **2 tablespoons chopped fresh parsley**

1. Remove lid from a 6-quart Instant Pot®. Press [Sauté]; use [Adjust] to select "More" mode. When the word "Hot" appears, swirl in oil. Add onion, carrot, parsnip, and garlic. Cook, stirring constantly, 5 minutes or until tender.

2. Add beans and next 6 ingredients (through bay leaf). Close and lock the lid of the Instant Pot®. Turn the steam release handle to "Venting" position. Press [Slow Cook], and use [Adjust] to select "Less" mode. Press [-] or [+] to choose 8 hours cook time.

3. Combine breadcrumbs, cheese, and butter in a small bowl; toss with a fork until moist. Stir breadcrumb mixture and sausage into bean mixture; sprinkle with parsley.

Moroccan Chickpea Tagine with Apricots

SERVES 6 - HANDS-ON: 10 MINUTES
SLOW COOK: 3 HOURS 30 MINUTES

This tagine is completely satisfying, even if you love meat, with nutty chickpeas and subtle spicing. Serve with harissa, fat-free yogurt, and lemon slices, if desired.

- **1 cup dried chickpeas (garbanzo beans)**
- **2½ cups vertically sliced onion**
- **2 cups organic lower-sodium vegetable stock**
- **1 cup water**
- **1 tablespoon grated peeled fresh ginger**
- **1½ teaspoons ground cumin**
- **½ teaspoon salt**
- **½ teaspoon ground cinnamon**
- **8 garlic cloves, minced**
- **8 dried apricots, halved**
- **4 medium carrots, cut into 1-inch pieces**
- **3 saffron threads, crushed**
- **1 (¾ x 3-inch) strip fresh lemon rind**
- **½ cup chopped fresh parsley**
- **¼ cup slivered almonds, toasted**
- **2 (8.8-ounce) pouches microwaveable pre-cooked whole-grain brown rice (such as Uncle Ben's Ready Rice)**

1. Sort and wash chickpeas; place in the inner pot of a 6-quart Instant Pot®. Cover with water to 2 inches above chickpeas; cover inner pot with aluminum foil, and let stand 8 hours. Drain chickpeas.

2. Combine drained chickpeas, onion, and next 11 ingredients (through lemon rind) in inner pot; stir well. Return inner pot to cooker. Close and lock the lid of the Instant Pot®. Turn the steam release handle to "Venting" position. Press [Slow Cook], and use [Adjust] to select "More" mode. Press [-] or [+] to choose 3 hours and 30 minutes cook time. (Cook additional time or until chickpeas are tender.) Sprinkle with parsley and almonds; discard lemon rind.

3. Heat rice according to package directions. Serve chickpea mixture over rice.

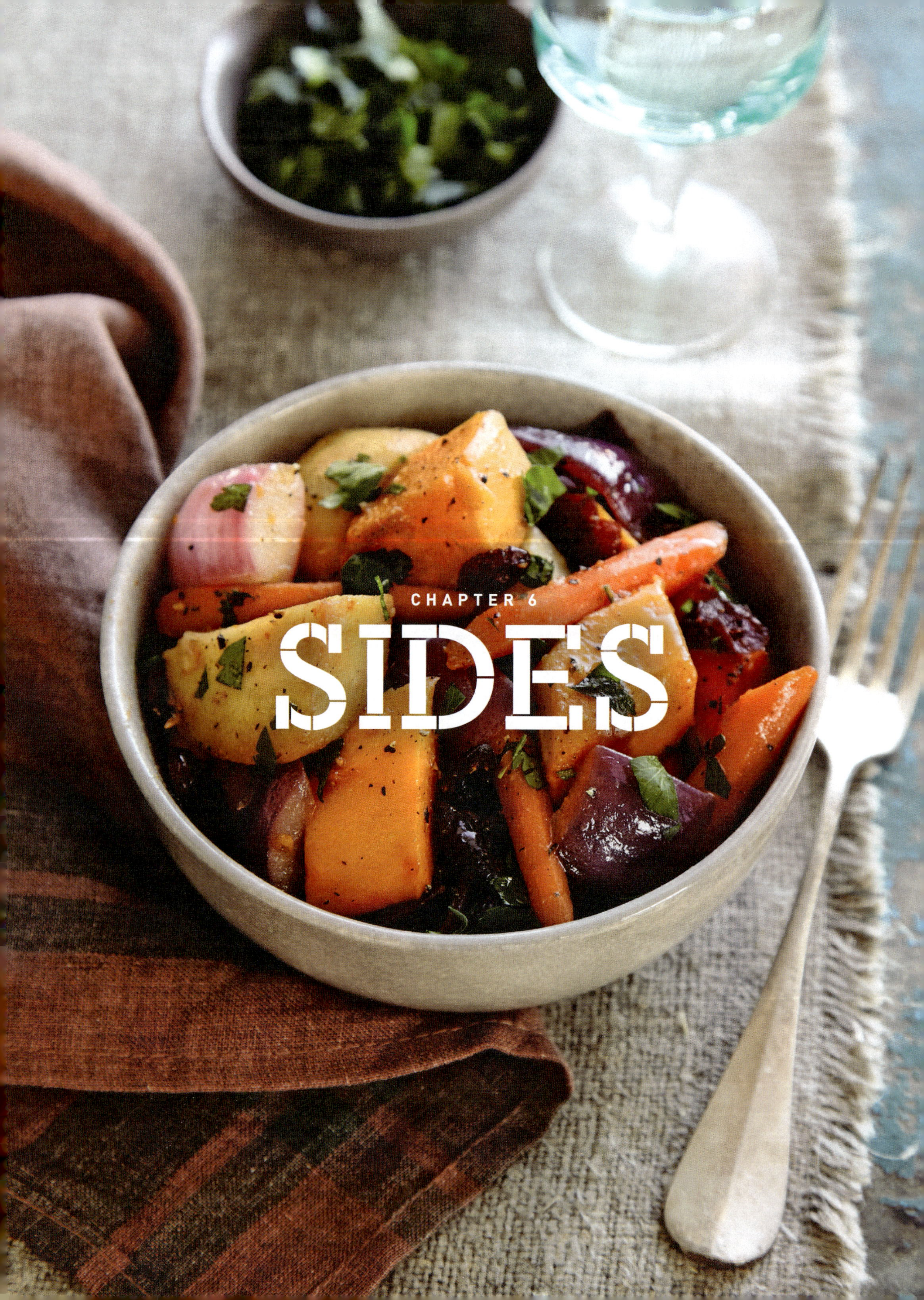

CHAPTER 6

SIDES

PRESSURE COOKER

Cauliflower and Fennel with Dijon-Cider Vinaigrette

SERVES 6 - HANDS-ON: 10 MINUTES
UNDER PRESSURE: 2 MINUTES

This simple side of cauliflower dressed in a vinaigrette may be just the ticket to get you past your childhood aversion to this veggie. The Dijon-cider vinaigrette is what really seals the deal.

- **1 large head cauliflower**
- **1 cup water**
- **1 cup sliced fennel**
- **¼ cup olive oil**
- **1 tablespoon chopped fresh fennel fronds**
- **2 tablespoons cider vinegar**
- **2 teaspoons Dijon mustard**
- **1 teaspoon honey**
- **¼ teaspoon kosher salt**
- **¼ teaspoon freshly ground black pepper**

1. Place cauliflower in a 6-quart Instant Pot®; add 1 cup water. Close and lock the lid of the Instant Pot®. Turn the steam release handle to "Sealing" position. Press [Manual]; select "High Pressure," and use [-] or [+] to choose 2 minutes pressure cooking time. When time is up, turn cooker off. Open the cooker using Quick Pressure Release (page 4). Chop cauliflower into florets. Toss with fennel.

2. Combine oil and remaining ingredients in a large bowl, stirring with a whisk. Add cauliflower mixture; toss to coat.

SWAP IN A SNAP!
For variation, try this recipe with broccoli rather than the cauliflower.

Creole Braised Cabbage

Collard Greens with Ham Hocks

PRESSURE COOKER

Creole Braised Cabbage

SERVES 14 - HANDS-ON: 15 MINUTES
UNDER PRESSURE: 12 MINUTES

- **4 center-cut bacon slices**
- **1 medium onion, chopped**
- **4 garlic cloves, minced**
- **1 (2-pound) head green cabbage, halved, cored, and cut into ¼-inch-thick slices (about 12 cups)**
- **⅔ cup fat-free, lower-sodium chicken broth**
- **2 teaspoons chopped fresh oregano**
- **2 teaspoons chopped fresh thyme**
- **½ teaspoon crushed red pepper**
- **¼ teaspoon freshly ground black pepper**
- **1 (14.5-ounce) can diced tomatoes with green pepper, celery, and onion, drained**
- **2 bay leaves**
- **¼ cup chopped fresh parsley**

1. Remove lid from a 6-quart Instant Pot®. Press [Sauté]; use [Adjust] to select "Normal" mode. Add bacon to cooker, and cook 7 minutes or until crisp. Remove bacon from inner pot, reserving 2 tablespoons drippings in pot; drain and crumble bacon. Add onion and garlic to drippings in pot; cook, stirring constantly, 4 minutes. Stir in cabbage; cook 2 minutes or until cabbage begins to wilt, stirring frequently. Stir in broth and next 6 ingredients (through bay leaves). Turn cooker off.

2. Close and lock the lid of the Instant Pot®. Turn the steam release handle to "Sealing" position. Press [Manual]; select "High Pressure," and use [-] or [+] to choose 3 minutes pressure cooking time. When time is up, turn cooker off. Open the cooker using Quick Pressure Release (page 4).

3. Remove bay leaves; discard. Stir in parsley and crumbled bacon.

PRESSURE COOKER

Collard Greens with Ham Hocks

SERVES 4 - HANDS-ON: 15 MINUTES
UNDER PRESSURE: 46 MINUTES

You will enjoy old-fashioned Southern flavor in these greens.

- **6 ounces smoked ham hocks**
- **2 cups water**
- **1 pound collard greens, stems removed and chopped**
- **1 tablespoon canola oil**
- **1 tablespoon chopped fresh garlic**
- **½ teaspoon salt**
- **¼ teaspoon freshly ground black pepper**
- **⅛ teaspoon crushed red pepper**
- **1 (14.5-ounce) can fat-free, lower-sodium chicken broth**
- **1 small onion, chopped**
- **1 tablespoon brown sugar**
- **1 tablespoon cider vinegar**

1. Combine ham hocks and water in a 6-quart Instant Pot®. Close and lock the lid of the Instant Pot®. Turn the steam release handle to "Sealing" position. Press [Manual]; select "High Pressure," and use [-] or [+] to choose 40 minutes pressure cooking time. When time is up, turn cooker off. Open the cooker using Quick Pressure Release (page 4).

2. Drain ham hocks; discard cooking liquid. Return inner pot to cooker; return ham to pot. Add greens and next 7 ingredients (through onion). Press [Manual]; select "High Pressure," and use [-] or [+] to choose 6 minutes pressure cooking time. When time is up, turn cooker off. Open the cooker using Quick Pressure Release (page 4).

3. Remove ham hocks; let stand until cool enough to handle. Remove ham from bones; coarsely chop. Discard bones, skin, and fat. Stir ham, brown sugar, and vinegar into greens.

SWAP IN A SNAP!
Canned diced tomatoes seasoned with garlic and onion or basil, garlic, and oregano work well in this recipe.

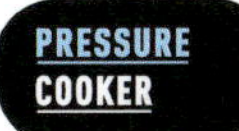

PRESSURE COOKER

Curried Carrots and Parsnips

SERVES 8 · HANDS-ON: 15 MINUTES
UNDER PRESSURE: 4 MINUTES

Fresh cilantro and golden raisins pair nicely with carrots and parsnips.

- **1 tablespoon olive oil**
- **1 pound carrots, peeled and cut into 1-inch pieces**
- **1 pound parsnips, peeled and cut into 1-inch pieces**
- **2 teaspoons curry powder**
- **1 teaspoon ground cumin**
- **¼ teaspoon ground cinnamon**
- **¼ teaspoon salt**
- **⅛ teaspoon ground red pepper**
- **1 cup organic vegetable broth**
- **½ cup golden raisins**
- **2 tablespoons chopped fresh cilantro**

1. Remove lid from a 6-quart Instant Pot®. Press [Sauté]; use [Adjust] to select "More" mode. When the word "Hot" appears, swirl in oil. Add carrots and next 6 ingredients (through red pepper). Cook, stirring constantly, 1 minute or until spices are lightly toasted. Stir in broth and raisins. Turn cooker off. Close and lock the lid of the Instant Pot®. Turn the steam release handle to "Sealing" position. Press [Manual]; select "High Pressure," and use [-] or [+] to choose 4 minutes pressure cooking time. When time is up, press [Cancel]. Open the cooker using Quick Pressure Release (page 4).

2. Remove vegetables from cooker with a slotted spoon, and place on a platter; discard cooking liquid. Sprinkle vegetables with cilantro.

PRESSURE COOKER

Bacon-Cider Turnips and Apples

SERVES 8 · HANDS-ON: 15 MINUTES
UNDER PRESSURE: 3 MINUTES

This sweet and savory side would be a delicious accompaniment to your next holiday dinner.

- **4 center-cut bacon slices**
- **2 pounds small turnips, peeled and each cut into 8 wedges (about 6 cups)**
- **1¾ cups vertically sliced onion**
- **2 Fuji apples, peeled and cut into wedges (about 1 pound)**
- **1 cup apple cider**
- **½ teaspoon salt**
- **½ teaspoon freshly ground black pepper**
- **2 tablespoons chopped fresh parsley**

1. Remove lid from a 6-quart Instant Pot®. Add bacon to inner pot. Press [Sauté]; use [Adjust] to select "Normal" mode. Cook bacon until crisp; remove from pot, and drain on paper towels. Add turnips, onion, and apple to drippings in inner pot; cook, stirring constantly, 2 minutes or until lightly browned. Stir in cider, salt, and pepper. Turn cooker off.

2. Close and lock the lid of the Instant Pot®. Turn the steam release handle to "Sealing" position. Press [Manual]; select "High Pressure," and use [-] or [+] to choose 3 minutes pressure cooking time. When time is up, turn cooker off. Open the cooker using Quick Pressure Release (page 4).

3. Place turnip mixture on a serving dish. Sprinkle with crumbled bacon and parsley.

SWAP IN A SNAP!
Use McIntosh apples instead of the Fuji.

Curried Carrots and Parsnips

Bacon-Cider Turnips and Apples

Garlic and Chive Mashed Potatoes

SERVES 5 - HANDS-ON: 8 MINUTES
UNDER PRESSURE: 9 MINUTES

Whole cloves of garlic simmer to a sweet tenderness along with the potatoes, and then melt right into the mash. Tangy Greek yogurt adds great flavor with very little fat. You can leave the peels on your potatoes for a more rustic mash, or peel for a smoother effect.

- **2 cups lower-sodium chicken stock**
- **2 pounds peeled Yukon gold or red potato, cut into 1-inch-thick slices**
- **4 garlic cloves, peeled**
- **1 cup plain fat-free Greek yogurt**
- **½ cup whole milk**
- **½ teaspoon salt**
- **¼ cup chopped fresh chives**

1. Combine first 3 ingredients in a 6-quart Instant Pot®. Close and lock the lid of the Instant Pot®. Turn the steam release handle to "Sealing" position. Press [Manual]; select "High Pressure," and use [-] or [+] to choose 9 minutes pressure cooking time. When time is up, turn cooker off. Open the cooker using Quick Pressure Release (page 4).

2. Mash potato mixture with a potato masher to desired consistency. Stir in yogurt, milk, and salt. Stir in chives just before serving.

Cheddar Mashed Potatoes

SERVES 9 - HANDS-ON: 14 MINUTES
UNDER PRESSURE: 9 MINUTES

- **2 pounds peeled russet potatoes, cut into ½-inch-thick slices**
- **1 cup water**
- **1 teaspoon salt**
- **1 teaspoon freshly ground black pepper**
- **4 ounces extra-sharp cheddar cheese, shredded (about 1 cup)**
- **¼ cup plus 2 tablespoons 2% reduced-fat milk**
- **½ cup chopped scallions**
- **2 tablespoons reduced-fat sour cream**
- **4 center-cut bacon slices, cooked and crumbled (drained)**

1. Place potato, 1 cup water, ½ teaspoon of the salt, and ½ teaspoon of the pepper in a 6-quart Instant Pot®. Close and lock the lid of the Instant Pot®. Turn the steam release handle to "Sealing" position. Press [Manual]; select "High Pressure," and use [-] or [+] to choose 9 minutes pressure cooking time. When time is up, turn cooker off. Open the cooker using Quick Pressure Release (page 4).

2. Add cheese and milk to potato mixture in cooker; mash to desired consistency. Press [Sauté]; use [Adjust] to select "Normal" mode. Cook, stirring constantly, 1 minute or until thoroughly heated. Stir in remaining ½ teaspoon salt, remaining ½ teaspoon pepper, scallions, sour cream, and bacon.

Rosemary Potato Wedges

SERVES 5 - HANDS-ON: 10 MINUTES
UNDER PRESSURE: 7 MINUTES

Stir the potatoes very frequently while sautéing to prevent sticking.

- **2 tablespoons olive oil**
- **1 pound small red potatoes, quartered**
- **1 cup organic vegetable broth**
- **2 teaspoons chopped fresh rosemary**
- **2 tablespoons grated fresh Parmesan cheese**
- **¼ teaspoon kosher salt**
- **¼ teaspoon freshly ground black pepper**

1. Remove lid from a 6-quart Instant Pot®. Press [Sauté]; use [Adjust] to select "More" mode. When the word "Hot" appears, swirl in 1 tablespoon of the oil. Add potatoes to cooker. Cook, stirring constantly, 5 minutes or until lightly browned. Add broth; sprinkle with rosemary. Turn cooker off.

2. Close and lock the lid of the Instant Pot®. Turn the steam release handle to "Sealing" position. Press [Manual]; select "High Pressure," and use [-] or [+] to choose 7 minutes pressure cooking time. When time is up, turn cooker off. Open the cooker using Quick Pressure Release (page 4). Drain potatoes, discarding cooking liquid.

3. Place potatoes in a large bowl. Add remaining 1 tablespoon oil, cheese, salt, and pepper; toss gently. Serve immediately.

SWAP IN A SNAP!
Any herb will work. Try basil, thyme, or parsley.

SLOW COOKER

Balsamic Root Vegetables

SERVES 8 - HANDS-ON: 20 MINUTES
SLOW COOK: 4 HOURS

For a delicious twist, add a sprinkling of cooked and crumbled bacon just before serving.

Cooking spray
1 pound parsnips, peeled and cut into 1½-inch pieces
1 pound carrots, cut into 1½-inch pieces
2 large red onions, coarsely chopped
¾ cup sweetened dried cranberries
1½ pounds sweet potatoes, peeled and cut into 1½-inch pieces
1 tablespoon light brown sugar
1 tablespoon olive oil
2 tablespoons balsamic vinegar
¾ teaspoon salt
½ teaspoon freshly ground black pepper
⅓ cup chopped fresh flat-leaf parsley

1. Coat the inner pot of a 6-quart Instant Pot® with cooking spray. Combine first 4 ingredients (through cranberries) in pot; layer sweet potatoes over top.

2. Combine sugar and next 4 ingredients (through pepper) in a small bowl, stirring with a whisk; pour over vegetable mixture. (Do not stir.)

3. Close and lock the lid of the Instant Pot®. Turn the steam release handle to "Venting" position. Press [Slow Cook], and use [Adjust] to select "More" mode. Press [-] or [+] to choose 4 hours cook time. (Cook additional time, if necessary, until vegetables are tender.) Toss with parsley just before serving.

Indian-Spiced Lentils

SERVES 9 - HANDS-ON: 8 MINUTES
SLOW COOK: 4 HOURS

We used small, dark green du Puy lentils, which cook faster than regular or black lentils and result in an earthy, warming meal.

1½ cups dried du Puy lentils
1 cup finely diced onion
6 cups water
3 tablespoons chopped peeled fresh ginger
2 teaspoons ground cumin
2 teaspoons ground coriander
1 teaspoon ground cinnamon
1 teaspoon ground cardamom
1 teaspoon ground turmeric
¾ teaspoon salt
¼ teaspoon ground cloves
¼ teaspoon ground red pepper
3 garlic cloves, minced
2 jalapeño peppers, minced

Combine all ingredients in the inner pot of a 6-quart Instant Pot®. Close and lock the lid of the Instant Pot®. Turn the steam release handle to "Venting" position. Press [Slow Cook], and use [Adjust] to select "Less" mode. Press [-] or [+] to choose 4 hours cook time.

Wild Rice, Fruit, and Pecan Pilaf

SERVES 7 - HANDS-ON: 7 MINUTES
SLOW COOK: 2 HOURS 15 MINUTES

This is a great holiday side dish to go alongside roast turkey or baked ham.

- **1 cup unseasoned wild and brown rice blend**
- **1 cup unsalted vegetable broth**
- **1 cup apple cider**
- **¼ cup minced shallots**
- **½ teaspoon salt**
- **⅓ cup chopped dried apricots**
- **⅓ cup golden raisins**
- **1 tablespoon sherry vinegar**
- **1 teaspoon finely chopped fresh sage**
- **¼ cup chopped pecans, toasted**

1. Combine first 5 ingredients (through salt) in the inner pot of a 6-quart Instant Pot®.

2. Close and lock the lid of the Instant Pot®. Turn the steam release handle to "Venting" position. Press [Slow Cook], and use [Adjust] to select "More" mode. Press [-] or [+] to choose 2 hours cook time. (Cook additional time, if necessary, until rice is tender.)

3. Remove lid. Stir in apricots and raisins. Close and lock lid, and let stand 15 minutes. Transfer rice mixture to a serving bowl. Stir in vinegar and sage; sprinkle with pecans before serving.

SLOW COOKER

Ratatouille with Basil

SERVES 16 - HANDS-ON: 12 MINUTES
SLOW COOK: 3 HOURS 30 MINUTES

Eggplant is usually prepared with lots of oil, which it soaks up like a sponge. In the Instant Pot®, a little bit of olive oil is all that is needed, and the moist heat makes the eggplant tender.

- **1 tablespoon extra-virgin olive oil**
- **2¼ cups chopped onion**
- **3 garlic cloves, chopped**
- **7 cups cubed peeled eggplant**
- **1¼ cups chopped red bell pepper**
- **1 cup chopped green bell pepper**
- **1½ cups tomato sauce**
- **1 teaspoon dried thyme**
- **½ teaspoon salt**
- **½ teaspoon freshly ground black pepper**
- **1 medium zucchini, quartered lengthwise and sliced (about 2 cups)**
- **1 medium-sized yellow squash, quartered lengthwise and sliced (about 2 cups)**
- **1 cup chopped fresh basil**
- **1 tablespoon balsamic vinegar**

1. Remove lid from a 6-quart Instant Pot®. Press [Sauté]; use [Adjust] to select "Normal" mode. When the word "Hot" appears, swirl in oil. Add onion and garlic; cook, stirring constantly, 5 minutes. Stir in eggplant and next 8 ingredients (through squash).

2. Close and lock the lid of the Instant Pot®. Turn the steam release handle to "Venting" position. Press [Slow Cook], and use [Adjust] to select "More" mode. Press [-] or [+] to choose 3 hours and 30 minutes cook time. Turn cooker off. Remove lid, and stir in basil and vinegar. Cool 1 hour. Serve at room temperature, or cover and store in refrigerator for up to 1 week.

SLOW COOKER

Wilted Baby Kale with Carmelized Onions

SERVES 6 - HANDS-ON: 5 MINUTES
SLOW COOK: 6 HOURS 30 MINUTES

- **Cooking spray**
- **4 cups vertically sliced Vidalia or other sweet onion**
- **1 tablespoon chopped fresh thyme**
- **1 tablespoon brown sugar**
- **2 tablespoons cider vinegar**
- **2 tablespoons water**
- **¼ teaspoon salt**
- **¼ teaspoon freshly ground black pepper**
- **2 garlic cloves, chopped**
- **½ teaspoon grated lemon rind**
- **2 (9-ounce) packages prewashed baby kale leaves and stems, coarsely chopped**
- **¼ cup sunflower seed kernels, toasted**

1. Coat the inner pot of a 6-quart Instant Pot® with cooking spray. Combine onion and next 7 ingredients (through garlic) in pot; toss well. Close and lock the lid of the Instant Pot®. Turn the steam release handle to "Venting" position. Press [Slow Cook], and use [Adjust] to select "Less" mode. Press [-] or [+] to choose 6 hours cook time. (Cook additional time, if necessary, or until onions are very soft and caramelized.) Stir in lemon rind and half of kale. Turn cooker off.

2. Press [Sauté], and use [Adjust] to select "More" mode. When mixture comes to a boil, cook 5 minutes. Turn cooker off. Stir in remaining half of kale.

3. Close and lock the lid of the Instant Pot®. Turn the steam release handle to "Venting" position. Press [Slow Cook], and use [Adjust] to select "More" mode. Press [-] or [+] to choose 30 minutes cook time. (Check kale for tenderness after 15 minutes.) Stir occasionally. Sprinkle with sunflower seed kernels before serving.

“Baked” Sweet Potato with Lime Butter

SERVES 6 - HANDS-ON: 10 MINUTES
SLOW COOK: 4 HOURS

Need to add choice and variety to your weeknight dinners? Just cook the potatoes, and let your family pick the buttery topping of their choice.

- **6 small sweet potatoes (about 2 pounds), scrubbed**
- **1⅓ cups water**
- **¼ cup whipped butter, softened**
- **1 garlic clove, minced**
- **¼ teaspoon grated lime rind**

1. Arrange potatoes in the inner pot of a 6-quart Instant Pot®. Add 1⅓ cups water to pot. Close and lock the lid of the Instant Pot®. Turn the steam release handle to "Venting" position. Press [Slow Cook], and use [Adjust] to select "Less" mode. Press [-] or [+] to choose 4 hours cook time. Remove potatoes from cooker; discard water.

2. Combine butter, garlic, and lime rind in a small bowl. Serve with potatoes.

HOT AND SMOKY BUTTER
Prepare potatoes according to step 1. Omit garlic and lime rind in butter mixture. Stir in ¼ teaspoon crushed red pepper and ½ teaspoon Spanish smoked paprika.

MAPLE-CINNAMON BUTTER
Prepare potatoes according to step 1. Omit garlic and lime rind in butter mixture. Stir in 1 tablespoon maple syrup and ½ teaspoon ground cinnamon.

CHAPTER 7

DESSERTS

Vanilla Bean Cheesecakes with Port-Cherry Sauce

SERVES 4 - HANDS-ON: 20 MINUTES
UNDER PRESSURE: 9 MINUTES

CHEESECAKES:

2 cups water
2 tablespoons sliced almonds, toasted
8 vanilla wafers
1 (3-inch) piece vanilla bean, split lengthwise
⅓ cup sugar
2 tablespoons all-purpose flour
3 tablespoons fat-free cream cheese
1 (8-ounce) block ⅓-less-fat cream cheese, softened
1 large egg

SAUCE:

½ cup frozen pitted dark sweet cherries
2 tablespoons sugar
1½ tablespoons ruby port or other sweet red wine
½ teaspoon cornstarch
2 teaspoons water

1. Make the cheesecakes: Pour 2 cups water into a 6-quart Instant Pot®. Place steam rack in bottom of inner pot; fold handles under rack. Place almonds and vanilla wafers in a food processor; process until finely ground. Divide almond mixture among ramekins, shaking gently to cover bottom of each ramekin. Scrape seeds from vanilla bean; discard bean. Place vanilla bean seeds, ⅓ cup sugar, and next 3 ingredients (through ⅓-less-fat cream cheese) in food processor; process 15 seconds or until smooth. Add egg; process 5 seconds or until blended. Scrape sides of bowl as needed. Divide cream cheese mixture among ramekins. Tightly cover each ramekin with a 9 x 5-inch piece of aluminum foil, tucking excess under bottom. Center 3 ramekins on the rack in a cloverleaf pattern; stack remaining ramekin in center of the cloverleaf.

2. Close and lock the lid of the Instant Pot®. Turn the steam release handle to "Sealing" position. Press [Manual]; select "High Pressure," and use [-] or [+] to choose 9 minutes pressure cooking time. When time is up, let stand 3 minutes. Open the cooker using Quick Pressure Release (page 4).

3. Cool cheesecakes slightly. Carefully remove ramekins from cooker; place on a wire rack. Let stand 40 minutes. Remove foil, and cover with plastic wrap. Chill at least 4 hours.

4. Make the sauce: Combine cherries, 2 tablespoons sugar, and port in a small saucepan. Bring to a boil over medium heat, stirring frequently; cook 2 to 3 minutes or until cherries thaw and sugar dissolves. Combine cornstarch and 2 teaspoons water in a small bowl, stirring with a whisk; add to cherry mixture. Return to a boil, and cook 1 minute or until slightly thick, stirring frequently. Serve cheesecakes with sauce.

Date-Walnut Bread Pudding

SERVES 8 · HANDS-ON: 20 MINUTES
UNDER PRESSURE: 34 MINUTES

Wearing lined rubber gloves gives you more dexterity than pot holders in removing the rack from the cooker.

- **4 large eggs, lightly beaten**
- **1¼ cups 2% reduced-fat milk**
- **¾ cup granulated sugar**
- **¼ cup packed brown sugar**
- **2 tablespoons orange-flavored liqueur**
- **1 teaspoon vanilla extract**
- **½ teaspoon ground cinnamon**
- **8 ounces French bread, cut into 1-inch cubes**
- **¾ cup chopped pitted Medjool dates**
- **½ cup chopped walnuts, toasted**
- **Cooking spay**
- **5½ cups water**
- **3 tablespoons water**
- **¼ cup half-and-half**

1. Combine eggs, milk, ¼ cup of the granulated sugar, brown sugar, and next 3 ingredients (through cinnamon) in a large bowl. Gently fold in bread, dates, and walnuts. Pour mixture into a 1½-quart soufflé dish coated with cooking spray. Cover with foil, making sure foil fits tightly around sides and under bottom of dish but leaving room for pudding to puff during cooking.

2. Place steam rack in inner pot of a 6-quart Instant Pot®; position handles upright. Carefully set dish on rack in cooker. Push dish to one side, and carefully pour 5½ cups water between dish and side of pot. Center dish on rack.

3. Close and lock the lid of the Instant Pot®. Turn the steam release handle to "Sealing" position. Press [Manual]; select "High Pressure," and use [-] or [+] to choose 34 minutes pressure cooking time. When time is up, turn cooker off. Open the cooker using Quick Pressure Release (page 4). Blot foil with a towel to remove any water that collected on top of the foil. Wearing lined rubber gloves, grasp the handles of the steam rack and carefully remove dish from cooker. Remove foil, and let stand 15 minutes.

4. While pudding stands, combine remaining ½ cup granulated sugar and 3 tablespoons water in a medium saucepan. Bring to a boil over medium heat (do not stir). Boil 4 minutes or until sugar mixture is amber, swirling pan occasionally. Remove from heat. Gradually add half-and-half, stirring with a whisk until smooth (be careful of hot steam). If necessary, return to low heat to dissolve caramel, stirring until smooth. Serve bread pudding with caramel sauce.

Pumpkin Pie Custards with Gingersnap Topping

SERVES 6 - HANDS-ON: 8 MINUTES
UNDER PRESSURE: 7 MINUTES

Be careful not to overcook these custards, as they will continue to cook even after they are removed from the pressure cooker.

- **3 large eggs, well beaten**
- **1¼ cups canned unsweetened pumpkin**
- **1 cup 2% reduced-fat evaporated milk**
- **1 teaspoon vanilla extract**
- **½ cup sugar**
- **¼ teaspoon salt**
- **¾ teaspoon ground cinnamon**
- **¼ teaspoon ground nutmeg**
- **¼ teaspoon ground ginger**
- **2 cups water**
- **½ cup frozen reduced-calorie whipped topping, thawed**
- **8 teaspoons crushed gingersnaps**

1. Beat eggs with a whisk until blended in a 2-quart measuring cup. Stir in pumpkin, milk, and vanilla. Combine sugar and next 4 ingredients (through ginger). Add to pumpkin mixture, stirring with a wire whisk. Pour pumpkin mixture evenly into 6 (6-ounce) ramekins or custard cups.

2. Pour 2 cups water into a 6-quart Instant Pot®. Fold handles under steam rack, and place steam rack in bottom of inner pot. Tightly cover each ramekin with a 9 x 5-inch piece of aluminum foil, tucking excess under bottom. Center 3 ramekins on the rack in a cloverleaf pattern; stack remaining 3 ramekins on top, offsetting the cloverleaf pattern for stability.

3. Close and lock the lid of the Instant Pot®. Turn the steam release handle to "Sealing" position. Press [Manual]; select "High Pressure," and use [-] or [+] to choose 7 minutes pressure cooking time. Open the cooker using Quick Pressure Release (page 4).

4. Carefully remove top 3 ramekins from the cooker; place on a wire rack, leaving foil on. Remove remaining 3 ramekins from cooker, and remove foil immediately. Let top 3 ramekins stand covered at least 10 minutes or until a thin sharp knife inserted in center through foil comes out clean; uncover and cool completely. Cover and chill at least 3 hours. Top each custard with whipped topping and gingersnaps just before serving.

Chocolate-Espresso Pudding Cake

SERVES 8 · HANDS-ON: 15 MINUTES
UNDER PRESSURE: 11 MINUTES

2 cups water
Cooking spray
5 tablespoons sugar
4 ounces bittersweet chocolate, chopped
2 tablespoons butter
⅓ cup (about 1.5 ounces) all-purpose flour
¼ cup unsweetened cocoa
¼ teaspoon salt
2 large eggs, separated
2 tablespoons coffee-flavored liqueur
2 teaspoons instant espresso granules
2 cups coffee or vanilla bean low-fat ice cream
Chocolate shavings (optional)

1. Pour 2 cups water into inner pot of a 6-quart Instant Pot®. Place the steam rack in inner pot; position handles upright. Coat a 6-inch round cake pan with cooking spray; sprinkle with 1 tablespoon of the sugar, shaking gently to coat bottom and sides of pan.

2. Combine chocolate and butter in a small microwave-safe bowl. Microwave at HIGH 30 to 45 seconds or until melted.

3. Weigh or lightly spoon flour into a dry measuring cup; level with a knife. Combine flour, cocoa, and salt in a small bowl. Beat egg whites with a mixer at high speed until soft peaks form; gradually add 2 tablespoons sugar, beating until stiff peaks form.

4. Combine egg yolks and remaining 2 tablespoons sugar in a large bowl. Beat with a mixer at high speed until thick and pale. Gradually beat in liqueur, espresso granules, and chocolate mixture. Fold beaten egg whites into egg yolk mixture. Gradually sift flour mixture into egg mixture, and fold in gently. Spoon batter into prepared pan, spreading gently (do not deflate batter). Cover with foil, making sure foil fits tightly around sides and under bottom of pan. Carefully set pan on rack in cooker.

5. Close and lock the lid of the Instant Pot®. Turn the steam release handle to "Sealing" position. Press [Manual]; select "High Pressure", and use [-] or [+] to choose 11 minutes pressure cooking time. When time is up, turn cooker off. Open the cooker using Quick Pressure Release (page 4). Remove pan from cooker using rack handles. Remove foil; cool 10 minutes. Spoon warm cake into bowls, and serve immediately with ice cream. Top with chocolate shavings, if desired.

PRESSURE COOKER

Pomegranate-Poached Pears

SERVES 6 - HANDS-ON: 14 MINUTES
UNDER PRESSURE: 3 MINUTES

The natural tartness of pomegranate juice brightens up the pears, while the sweet sour cream mixture adds richness.

- **6 firm ripe medium pears with stems**
- **1½ tablespoons fresh lemon juice**
- **1¾ cups pomegranate juice**
- **⅓ cup dried tart cherries**
- **6 tablespoons granulated sugar**
- **1 teaspoon vanilla extract**
- **2 (3-inch) cinnamon sticks, broken in half**
- **2 whole cloves**
- **¾ cup light sour cream**
- **4 teaspoons brown sugar**

1. Peel pears, leaving stems intact. Scoop bottom of core from each pear using the large end of a melon baller. With the small end, scoop out the seeds. If necessary, cut about ¼ inch from base of pears so they will sit flat. Squeeze lemon juice over pears.

2. Combine pomegranate juice and next 5 ingredients (through cloves) in a 6-quart Instant Pot®. Place pears, stem ends up, in inner pot.

3. Close and lock the lid of the Instant Pot®. Turn the steam release handle to "Sealing" position. Press [Manual]; select "High Pressure," and use [-] or [+] to choose 3 minutes pressure cooking time. When time is up, turn cooker off. Open the cooker using Quick Pressure Release (page 4).

4. Remove pears with a slotted spoon, and place on a rimmed serving platter. Press [Sauté]; use [Adjust] to select "More" mode. Bring cooking liquid to a boil, and cook until reduced to 1 cup (about 10 minutes). Remove and discard cinnamon sticks and cloves.

5. While cooking liquid boils, combine sour cream and brown sugar in a small bowl, stirring until brown sugar dissolves. Spoon pomegranate sauce over pears, and serve with sour cream mixture.

Marsala-Poached Pears

SERVES 8 - HANDS-ON: 13 MINUTES
SLOW COOK: 2 HOURS 30 MINUTES

An elegant, Italian cuisine-inspired dessert, this is ideal for a fall or winter meal. Use a melon baller to core the pears from the bottom (rather than cutting them in half first) so they can be served whole.

- **3 cups sweet Marsala or Madeira**
- **1 cup water**
- **¼ cup turbinado sugar or granulated sugar**
- **4 (3 x 1-inch) strips orange rind**
- **1 (3-inch) cinnamon stick**
- **8 peeled firm Bosc pears (about 3 pounds), cored**
- **8 teaspoons Gorgonzola dolce cheese**

1. Combine first 5 ingredients (through cinnamon stick) in a 6-quart Instant Pot®; arrange pears in cooker. Close and lock the lid of the Instant Pot®. Turn the steam release handle to "Venting" position. Press [Slow Cook], and use [Adjust] to select "Less" mode. Press [-] or [+] to choose 2 hours cook time. Carefully remove pears from cooker; cool.

2. While pears cool, pour cooking liquid into a 2-quart saucepan. Cook over medium-high heat until reduced to 2 cups (about 30 minutes). Discard cinnamon stick and orange rind strips. Serve pears with cooking liquid and cheese.

Tropical Bananas Foster

SERVES 7 · HANDS-ON: 5 MINUTES
SLOW COOK: 1 HOUR 15 MINUTES

Sliced bananas and cubed pineapple meet soft vanilla ice cream and a smooth cinnamon-flavored sauce to give you one decadent dessert.

- **Cooking spray**
- **½ cup packed dark brown sugar**
- **3 tablespoons butter**
- **¼ cup light coconut milk**
- **¼ cup dark rum**
- **1 cup (1-inch) cubed fresh pineapple**
- **¼ teaspoon ground cinnamon**
- **4 ripe bananas, cut into ½-inch-thick slices**
- **1¾ cups gluten-free vanilla reduced-fat ice cream**

1. Coat the inner pot of a 6-quart Instant Pot® with cooking spray. Combine brown sugar and next 3 ingredients (through rum) in pot. Close and lock the lid of the Instant Pot®. Turn the steam release handle to "Venting" position. Press [Slow Cook], and use [Adjust] to select "Less" mode. Press [-] or [+] to choose 1 hour cook time. Stir with a whisk until smooth.

2. Add pineapple, cinnamon, and banana to sauce, stirring to coat. Close and lock the lid of the Instant Pot®. Turn the steam release handle to "Venting" position. Press [Slow Cook], and use [Adjust] to select "Less" mode. Press [-] or [+] to choose 30 minutes cook time. (Turn off cooker after 15 minutes.) Serve immediately over ice cream.

Chocolate Bread Pudding

SERVES 10 - HANDS-ON: 10 MINUTES
SLOW COOK: 1 HOUR 30 MINUTES

Cooking spray
12 (1.3-ounce) slices sandwich bread, cut into 1½- to 2-inch pieces
5 large eggs, lightly beaten
½ cup sugar
¼ cup unsweetened cocoa, sifted
1 teaspoon vanilla extract
½ teaspoon salt
2 cups whole milk
½ cup semisweet chocolate mini-chips

1. Remove the inner pot of a 6-quart Instant Pot® from cooker, and coat with cooking spray. Place bread in pot.

2. Combine eggs and next 4 ingredients (through salt) in a large bowl; stir with a whisk. Gradually add milk, stirring with a whisk. Pour milk mixture over bread in cooker, pressing gently with a spoon to coat all bread pieces.

3. Tear off a 10½-inch-long piece of aluminum foil; lay foil on top of inner pot, gently smoothing it down the side of the pot. Trim pointed corners even with the rest of the foil, and tightly tuck it in under the rim.

4. Cut 1 (1¼-inch-long) slit in foil about 1 inch from edge with a thin, sharp knife. Cut a second 1¼-inch-long slit parallel to and about 1 inch to the inside of the first. Repeat this procedure 3 times, creating 2 concentric slits in foil at intervals of 12, 3, 6, and 9 o'clock. Place inner pot in cooker.

5. Close and lock the lid of the Instant Pot®. Turn the steam release handle to "Venting" position. Press [Slow Cook], and use [Adjust] to select "More" mode. Press [-] or [+] to choose 1 hour 30 minutes cook time. (Cook additional time, if necessary, or until a knife inserted in center comes out clean.) Carefully remove foil from inner pot to keep condensation from dripping onto pudding. Uncover and sprinkle with chocolate mini-chips. Cool 5 minutes before serving.

Brandied Plum-Vanilla Bread Pudding

SERVES 8 - HANDS-ON: 10 MINUTES
SLOW COOK: 1 HOUR 30 MINUTES

Brandy-spiked dried plums bejewel this delicious vanilla-infused bread pudding, putting a decadent spin on comfort food. Be sure to use moist, plump prunes for best results. Serve with a warm caramel sauce, if desired.

- **¾ cup pitted dried plums, quartered**
- **⅓ cup brandy**
- **1½ cups 2% reduced-fat milk**
- **½ cup sugar**
- **1 tablespoon vanilla extract**
- **1 teaspoon grated fresh lemon rind**
- **⅛ teaspoon salt**
- **3 large eggs, lightly beaten**
- **6 cups (1-inch) cubed day-old French bread (about 8 ounces)**
- **Cooking spray**

1. Combine plums and brandy in a bowl; let stand 30 minutes. Strain mixture through a sieve into a bowl, reserving soaking liquid and plums.

2. Combine reserved soaking liquid, milk, and next 5 ingredients (through eggs) in a large bowl, stirring well with a whisk. Add bread, tossing gently to coat. Stir in plums. Coat the inner pot of a 6-quart Instant Pot® with cooking spray. Spoon mixture into cooker.

3. Tear off a 10½-inch-long piece of aluminum foil; lay foil on top of inner pot, gently smoothing it down the side of the pot. Trim pointed corners even with the rest of the foil, and tightly tuck it in under the rim.

4. Cut 1 (1¼-inch-long) slit in foil about 1 inch from edge with a thin, sharp knife. Cut a second 1¼-inch-long slit parallel to and about 1 inch to the inside of the first. Repeat this procedure 3 times, creating 2 concentric slits in foil at intervals of 12, 3, 6, and 9 o'clock. Set inner pot inside cooker. Let stand 30 minutes.

5. Close and lock the lid of the Instant Pot®. Turn the steam release handle to "Venting" position. Press [Slow Cook], and use [Adjust] to select "More" mode. Press [-] or [+] to choose 1 hour 30 minutes cook time. (Cook additional time, if necessary, or until a knife inserted in center comes out clean.) Carefully remove foil from inner pot to keep condensation from dripping onto pudding. Let stand 10 minutes before serving.

SLOW COOKER

Chai, Mango, and Brown Rice Pudding

SERVES 5 - HANDS-ON: 9 MINUTES
SLOW COOK: 3 HOURS

Make sure that you use medium or short-grain rice; a longer grain does not have the same starches to thicken the pudding.

- **1 cup uncooked short-grain brown rice**
- **2½ cups water**
- **¼ cup chopped crystallized ginger**
- **¼ cup packed light brown sugar**
- **1 teaspoon ground cinnamon**
- **1 teaspoon vanilla extract**
- **¼ teaspoon ground fennel seeds**
- **⅛ teaspoon ground cardamom**
- **⅛ teaspoon ground cloves**
- **1/16 teaspoon salt**
- **1 (13.66-ounce) can light coconut milk**
- **1 cup chopped peeled mango (about 1 large)**
- **Additional ground cinnamon (optional)**

1. Combine all ingredients except mango in the inner pot of a 6-quart Instant Pot®; stir well.

2. Close and lock the lid of the Instant Pot®. Turn the steam release handle to "Venting" position. Press [Slow Cook], and use [Adjust] to select "More" mode. Press [-] or [+] to choose 3 hours cook time. Uncover and cool 1 hour. Serve at room temperature, or cover and chill. Top with mango before serving. Sprinkle with additional cinnamon, if desired.

Spiced Carrot Cake

SERVES 8 - HANDS-ON: 10 MINUTES
SLOW COOK: 1 HOUR 30 MINUTES

This cake is perfect with tea or coffee.

CAKE:

- **1 cup (about 4.5 ounces) all-purpose flour**
- **Cooking spray**
- **⅓ cup golden raisins**
- **⅓ cup granulated sugar**
- **⅓ cup packed light brown sugar**
- **1 teaspoon baking soda**
- **1 teaspoon ground cinnamon**
- **¼ teaspoon salt**
- **¼ teaspoon ground ginger**
- **¼ teaspoon grated whole nutmeg**
- **⅛ teaspoon ground cloves**
- **⅛ teaspoon ground allspice**
- **⅓ cup canola oil**
- **1 teaspoon vanilla extract**
- **2 large eggs, lightly beaten**
- **1½ cups finely shredded carrot**
- **1 cup water**

FROSTING:

- **3 ounces ⅓-less-fat cream cheese, softened**
- **½ cup powdered sugar**
- **½ teaspoon vanilla extract**

1. To make the cake: Lightly spoon flour into a dry measuring cup; level with a knife. Coat an 8-inch round (thin-rimmed) cake pan with cooking spray. Line cake pan with parchment paper; coat parchment paper with cooking spray, and dust with 1 tablespoon of the flour. Combine raisins and a second tablespoon of the flour in a small bowl; toss well.

2. Combine remaining flour, granulated sugar, and next 8 ingredients (through allspice) in a large bowl; stir with a whisk. Combine oil, vanilla, and eggs in a small bowl; add to flour mixture, stirring until blended. Stir in carrot and raisins. Pour batter into prepared pan.

3. Remove inner pot from a 6-quart Instant Pot®. Place steam rack in inner pot; fold handles under rack. Pour 1 cup water into pot, and place prepared pan on rack.

4. Tear off a 10½-inch-long piece of aluminum foil; lay foil on top of inner pot, gently smoothing it down the side of the pot. Trim pointed corners even with the rest of the foil, and tightly tuck it in under the rim.

5. Cut 1 (1¼-inch-long) slit in foil about 1 inch from edge with a thin, sharp knife. Cut a second 1¼-inch-long slit parallel to and about 1 inch to the inside of the first. Repeat this procedure 3 times, creating 2 concentric slits in foil at intervals of 12, 3, 6, and 9 o'clock. Set inner pot inside cooker.

6. Close and lock the lid of the Instant Pot®. Turn the steam release handle to "Venting" position. Press [Slow Cook], and use [Adjust] to select "More" mode. Press [-] or [+] to choose 1 hour 30 minutes cook time. (Cook additional time, if necessary, until a wooden pick inserted in center comes out clean.) Carefully remove lid from Instant Pot®. Blot any water that has collected on top of foil with a towel. Carefully remove foil from inner pot, so as to keep condensation from dripping onto cake. Transfer pan to a wire rack. Lightly blot top of cake with a paper towel, if necessary, to remove any collected moisture. Cool 10 minutes in pan on a wire rack; remove from pan. Cool completely on wire rack.

7. To make the frosting: Beat cream cheese with a mixer at medium speed until smooth; add powdered sugar and vanilla, beating until smooth. Garnish slices of cake with frosting.

Dulce de Leche Flan

SERVES 8 - HANDS-ON: 15 MINUTES
SLOW COOK: 2 HOURS 30 MINUTES

- **¾ cup sugar**
- **2 large eggs**
- **4 large egg yolks**
- **¾ cup canned fat-free dulce de leche or Homemade Dulce de Leche (recipe follows)**
- **½ cup 1% low-fat milk**
- **1 teaspoon vanilla extract**
- **¼ teaspoon salt**
- **1 (12-ounce) can evaporated fat-free milk**
- **5½ cups hot water**
- **Whipped cream, blackberries, raspberries, mint sprigs (optional)**

1. Place ½ cup of the sugar in a small skillet. Cook over medium heat 5 to 6 minutes or until amber in color (gently shaking pan occasionally until sugar melts). Remove from heat, and carefully pour hot caramel into a 1½-quart soufflé dish, tilting dish to coat bottom. Let stand 10 minutes.

2. Combine eggs and egg yolks in a large bowl; stir with a whisk. Add remaining ¼ cup sugar, ¾ cup dulce de leche, and next 4 ingredients (through evaporated milk), stirring until blended. Pour through a wire-mesh strainer over caramel in dish; discard solids. Cover dish with aluminum foil. Place steam rack in inner pot of a 6-quart Instant Pot® with handles in the upright position. Carefully set dish on rack in cooker.

3. Push dish to one side, and carefully pour 5½ cups hot water through the space created into the inner pot. Center dish on rack.

4. Close and lock the lid of the Instant Pot®. Turn the steam release handle to "Venting" position. Press [Slow Cook], and use [Adjust] to select "More" mode. Press [-] or [+] to choose 2 hours 30 minutes cook time. (When time is up, flan should be set, and a sharp knife inserted in center should come out clean. Recover dish, and cook additional time, if necessary.) Remove lid from cooker. Blot excess moisture from top of foil, if necessary, with a towel. Remove foil from dish.

5. Remove dish from cooker by carefully lifting out rack by the handles. Let stand on the rack until completely cool (about 1½ hours). Cover with foil, and chill at least 6 hours. Loosen edges of flan with a knife or rubber spatula. Place a plate upside down on top of pan; invert flan onto plate. Serve with whipped cream, blackberries, raspberries, and mint sprigs, if desired.

Homemade Dulce de Leche

SERVES 10 - HANDS-ON: 3 MINUTES
SLOW COOK: 9 HOURS

Making your own dulce de leche is incredibly easy, and the flavor is superior to the store-bought version. You'll have a little left over when you make the flan, so serve it over ice cream or as a dip for apple or banana slices.

- **1 (14-ounce) can fat-free sweetened condensed milk**

1. Pour milk into a 2-cup glass measuring cup; cover with aluminum foil. Place steam rack in inner pot of the Instant Pot®. Set measuring cup on rack. Carefully pour in very hot water to reach level of milk in measuring cup.

2. Close and lock the lid of the Instant Pot®. Turn the steam release handle to "Venting" position. Press [Slow Cook], and use [Adjust] to select "Less" mode. Press [-] or [+] to choose 9 hours cook time. Cook additional time, if necessary, until milk is caramel colored.

SLOW COOKER

Vanilla Bean Baked Custard

SERVES 4 - HANDS-ON: 10 MINUTES
SLOW COOK: 2 HOURS

This creamy custard is about as simple and delicious as it gets. Using evaporated milk helps the custard stabilize and not curdle.

- **1 (12-ounce) can evaporated low-fat milk**
- **½ cup 1% low-fat milk**
- **1 teaspoon vanilla bean paste**
- **1 large egg, lightly beaten**
- **2 large egg yolks**
- **⅓ cup sugar**
- **Cooking spray**
- **5½ cups hot water**
- **Raspberries and blueberries (optional)**

1. Combine milks in a medium saucepan. Bring to a simmer over medium heat, about 4 minutes. Remove from heat; add vanilla bean paste, stirring with a whisk until blended.

2. Combine egg, egg yolks, and sugar in a medium bowl, stirring with a whisk until blended. Gradually add hot milk, stirring vigorously with a whisk. Pour egg mixture through a sieve into a 1½-quart soufflé dish or ramekins coated with cooking spray; discard solids. Cover dish with aluminum foil.

3. Place steam rack in inner pot of a 6-quart Instant Pot® with handles in the upright position. Carefully set dish on rack in cooker.

4. Push dish to one side, and carefully pour 5½ cups hot water through the space created into the inner pot. Center dish on rack.

5. Close and lock the lid of the Instant Pot®. Turn the steam release handle to "Venting" position. Press [Slow Cook], and use [Adjust] to select "More" mode. Press [-] or [+] to choose 2 hours cook time. (When time is up, custard should be set, and a sharp knife inserted in center should come out clean. Recover dish, and cook additional time, if necessary.) Remove lid from cooker. Blot excess moisture from top of foil, if necessary, with a towel. Remove foil from dish.

6. Remove dish from cooker by carefully lifting out rack by the handles. Let stand on the rack until completely cool (about 1½ hours). Cover with foil, and chill at least 6 hours. Serve with blueberries and raspberries if desired.

METRIC EQUIVALENTS

LIQUID INGREDIENTS BY VOLUME

¼ tsp			=	1 ml
½ tsp			=	2 ml
1 tsp			=	5 ml
3 tsp =	1 Tbsp	=	½ fl oz =	15 ml
	2 Tbsp =	⅛ cup =	1 fl oz =	30 ml
	4 Tbsp =	¼ cup =	2 fl oz =	60 ml
	5⅓ Tbsp =	⅓ cup =	3 fl oz =	80 ml
	8 Tbsp =	½ cup =	4 fl oz =	120 ml
	10⅔ Tbsp =	⅔ cup =	5 fl oz =	160 ml
	12 Tbsp =	¾ cup =	6 fl oz =	180 ml
	16 Tbsp =	1 cup =	8 fl oz =	240 ml
	1 pt =	2 cups =	16 fl oz =	480 ml
	1 qt =	4 cups =	32 fl oz =	960 ml
			33 fl oz =	1000 ml = 1 l

DRY INGREDIENTS BY WEIGHT

(To convert ounces to grams, multiply the number of ounces by 30.)

1 oz	=1/16 lb	=30 g
4 oz	=¼ lb	=120 g
8 oz	=½ lb	=240 g
12 oz	=¾ lb	=360 g
16 oz	=1 lb	=480 g

EQUIVALENTS FOR DIFFERENT TYPES OF INGREDIENTS

STANDARD CUP	FINE POWDER (ex. flour)	GRAIN (ex. rice)	GRANULAR (ex. sugar)	LIQUID SOLIDS (ex. butter)	LIQUID (ex. milk)
1	140 g	150 g	190 g	200 g	240 ml
3/4	105 g	113 g	143 g	150 g	180 ml
2/3	93 g	100 g	125 g	133 g	160 ml
1/2	70 g	75 g	95 g	100 g	120 ml
1/3	47 g	50 g	63 g	67 g	80 ml
1/4	35 g	38 g	48 g	50 g	60 ml
1/8	18 g	19 g	24 g	25 g	30 ml

COOKING/OVEN TEMPERATURES AT SEA LEVEL

	FAHRENHEIT	CELSIUS	GAS MARK
FREEZE WATER	32° F	0° C	
ROOM TEMPERATURE	68° F	20° C	
BOIL WATER	212° F	100° C	
BAKE	325° F	160° C	3
	350° F	180° C	4
	375° F	190° C	5
	400° F	200° C	6
	425° F	220° C	7
	450° F	230° C	8
BROIL			GRILL

Published by Oxmoor House, an imprint of Time Inc. Books
225 Liberty Street, New York, NY 10281.

Printed in the United States of America.

EDITORIAL DIRECTOR Anja Schmidt
RECIPE EDITOR Julie Christopher
PROJECT EDITOR Lacie Pinyan
PHOTO EDITOR Paden Reich
ASSISTANT EDITOR Helena Joseph
EDITORIAL ASSISTANT Nicole Fisher
SENIOR DESIGNER Melissa Clark
DESIGNER Cathy Robbins
JUNIOR DESIGNER AnnaMaria Jacob
PHOTOGRAPHERS Robbie Caponetto, Alison Miksch, Victor Protasio, Hector Manuel Sanchez
PROP STYLISTS Kay E. Clarke, Claire Spollen
PROP COORDINATOR Audrey Davis
FOOD STYLIST Margaret Monroe Dickey
SENIOR PRODUCTION MANAGER Greg A. Amason
ASSISTANT PRODUCTION MANAGER Diane Rose Keener
ASSISTANT PRODUCTION AND PROJECT MANAGER Kelsey Smith
COPY EDITOR Jasmine Hodges
PROOFREADER Adrienne Davis
FELLOW Kyle Grace Mills

AT YOUR SERVICE

To send a comment or question, write to:
Oxmoor House Special Editions
4100 Old Montgomery Hwy., 4th Floor
Birmingham, AL 35209

INTERESTED IN MORE OXMOOR HOUSE COOKBOOKS?

Find a variety of titles from your favorite brands—Southern Living, Cooking Light, and many more. Whether you enjoy cooking, gardening, or decorating, you'll find a wealth of how-to books that can be shipped straight to your door. Please visit **timeincbooks.com** for our many special offers, or call 1.800.491.0551.

To search, savor, and share thousands of recipes, visit **myrecipes.com.**

RECIPE INDEX

Made in the USA
Lexington, KY
12 March 2017